Quotes from the North West Evening Mail

“Over 4000 people have now scaled the heights of Everest to stand on the world’s highest mountain. In contrast, only 424 people have rowed across the Atlantic Ocean from East to West in a pairs ocean rowing boat.”

“When Norman and James Beech arrive at La Gomera in December, they will be prepared for the biggest adventure of their lives. The team will have prepared for the challenge for two years by the time their 24 foot rowing boat hits the second largest piece of water on the earth’s surface.”

“No matter how much time you spend on your rowing machine, the real test is how you cope with being on the open water for the couple of months it is going to take.”

The Atlantic Job

A Dad and a Lad

Norman & James Beech

Filament Publishing

Filament Publishing Ltd
16, Croydon Road, Waddon
Croydon, Surrey. CR0 4PA
Telephone 020 8688 2598
info@filamentpublishing.com

www.filamentpublishing.com

Printed in the UK by the Berforts Group
Stevenage and Hastings

ISBN 978-1-905493-75-3

Special recognition and thanks to Christine and Lydia.

Your love and support throughout the preparations,

the row and the return home was quite amazing.

It always is!

Thank you for believing in us

and allowing us to go to sea.

You are both wonderful!

The Atlantic Job is dedicated to you.

In support of WaterAid

WaterAid uses practical solutions to provide clean water, safe sanitation and hygiene education to the world's poorest people.

- **884 million people** in the world do not have access to safe water. This is roughly **one in eight** of the world's population. (WHO/UNICEF)
- **2.6 billion people** in the world do not have access to adequate sanitation. This is almost **two-fifths** of the world's population. (WHO/UNICEF)
- **1.4 million children** die every year from diarrhoea caused by unclean water and poor sanitation. That's **4,000 child deaths a day or one child every 20 seconds**.
- This equates to **160 infant school classrooms** lost every single day to an entirely preventable public health crisis. (WHO/WaterAid)

'Beech Boys Atlantic' row supports the work of WaterAid. The story of the 'Beech Boys' as told in 'The Atlantic Job - A Dad and a Lad' was written with the aim of supporting WaterAid. After publishing and distribution costs, the proceeds from the sale of this book are all donated to WaterAid. WaterAid works in 26 countries in Africa, Asia and the Pacific region.

WaterAid's website gives full details of their work:
www.wateraid.org/uk/

Acknowledgements

We are very aware of all the help we have received to make the voyage possible. We would like to gratefully acknowledge the support we have received from:

Our family - Beechs, Morrows, Murrays, Scotts , McGraths
and our friends
University of Birmingham Sport
The Raymond Priestley Centre staff
University of Birmingham School of Sport & Exercise Science
University of Birmingham School of Manufacturing & Mechanical Engineering

Our sponsors (in alphabetical order)

Be-Well Foods
Birmingham Business School
Buffera Headwear
Bunches
Coolboard
COOLpilates
Coniston Corporate UK
Coniston Crusaders
Coniston and Torver FairTrade

Sponsors continued

Cotswold Outdoor
Creative Confectionery
Derwent Water Marina
Dorset Cereals
Exide Batteries
Expedition Foods
Furness Plastics
Gill Marine
Goacher Sails
Hadwins, Lakeland Land Rover
International Paint
John Ruskin School, Coniston
Lakes Leisure, Ulverston
Newman University College Birmingham
NPW
Pennington C of E School
PowerBar
River Deep, Mountain High
Sunshine Solar
The Coniston & Coppermines Cottages
University of Birmingham Metallurgy and Materials Department
University of Birmingham Sport
W. McClure Ltd

Key people and organisations

BBC Radio Cumbria

Blyth Workcats

Communities of Coniston and Torver in Cumbria

Coniston Branch Staff, Barclays Bank

Expert boat fitting out skills from Mike Stather, Jason Hadwin and Don Edmondsen

Family support team, Pat Menzies and Caroline Beckett

ITN Border and Tyne Tees television

John Ruskin Museum, Coniston

Mactra Marine

Marine Electrical Services

North West Evening Mail

Rowers at Greens Gym, Sheffield

WaterAid

Westmorland Gazette

Woodvale Challenge Ltd

Other donors and people who helped us

All the ocean rowers in the Woodvale Atlantic Race 2009

Angela Dawson

Asker Jeukendrup

Craig Holloway

Cumbrae Parish Church

Dan Turner

James Duguid

Jenn Cumming

Kates Skates

Taff and Karin Bowles

Wendy Yates and Alastair Boston

It is almost guaranteed that we will miss someone from the list of names. So to everyone who has followed our progress, e-mailed us encouraging messages, made a donation to assist the project, or donated directly to WaterAid. We are thankful for your support and for enabling this all to happen!

Special Note - throughout the row our friend Johan Hoving kept us up to date with crucial weather news. Talking with Johan after the row we learned of the dilemma he faced on a number of occasions when he could see the possibility of more bad weather hitting us, but it was perhaps a week away and he didn't want to burden us with worries that perhaps would have no substance if the low pressure took a different course and passed north of us. On one occasion Johan was working in Scotland running a winter mountaineering course. In order to get a signal to send us a weather update, he had to stand outside in the dark in sub-zero temperatures. We received his message in conditions some 50 degrees hotter than he was experiencing! Thanks Johan!

The names that went with us across the Atlantic were

Christine Beech
Lydia Beech
Jim and Minnie Morrow
Corinne Beech
Norman, Pauline, Stuart and Amy Murray
Lorraine and David McGrath
Gill, Mike, Katie and Hannah Scott
Laura Graham
John and Dorothy Harrison
The Jacqueline Clark Group
The Callaghan Family - Pat, Roz, Betty, Maeve and Mikey
Garry and Sue Tungate
The Farrow family - Andy, Claire, Daniel and Jonah
The Seeley family - Chris, Steph, Anna, Mark and Katie
Phil and Barbara Viney
Denise and Mike Wardale
Greg and Debbie Moon
Steve and Katie
Ken and Rita Orgill
Zena Wooldridge
Coniston Primary School
Ann Hall
Randall Williams
Geoff Pringle
Hugh and Kathleen Barr
Hilary Richardson

The Wood family - Woody and Sue, Billy, Joe and Daisy
Don and Kay Shepherd, James, Sarah, Matthew and Ben Foskett
Andy and Jen Ward
Paul Davis and Gina Lord
Roy and Gill Lake
Les and Molly Higgins
Albert Potts
Jenny Tancock
South Lakeland District Council
Rich, Becs, Rachael, Jessie and Ben Ensoll
John Kerr
Coniston Parish Council
Erica, Ian and Faye Caswell
Rob and Madeline Gee
Adam Walker
Colin, Katie, Jason, Gareth and Sarah Hodgson
Lewis Family
Chris Thomas
Jane, Paul, Amelie, Libby and Lara Jones
Brian and Janet Jacks
Kirkstone and Ambleside Rotary Club
Jiri Kuhn Gymnasium Nymburk Czech Republic
Bohuslav Sykora Living English Nymburk Czech Republic
Gabriella, Lucia, Francesca, Rhianna, Erin
Shelfield Community Academy
Glyn School
Peter, Pam and Charlotte Gale
Jati Salh

Ian, Deb, Hannah and Helena Wilding
Rudy, Helene, Rachel, Lewis and Mark Jackson
Steve and Mandy Simmonds
Doug and Gilly Potkin
The Priorsfield Society
Rachel Mills, Dan, Ben and Dave Sanderson
Kevin, Cathy, Jenni and Elliott Smith
Peter and Moira Bell
Keith, Ally, Craig and Katie Gibson
Andy, Emma, Lucy, Amy, Sophie Brennan
CCCC Holloway
Nicholson Outdoors
Ship Inn, Coniston
David Jackson
Debbie, Alexander and Christian Claydon
Dan Kelly and Family
Andy Cribb
Richard and Susan Simpson
Nicky Smith
BASLC Group B
Sir John Barrow School
Don Edmondson
Julie Flanagan
Janet Vickers
Vicky McDougall
Emma Holland and Mark Fairhurst
Mike Stather
Sandside Lodge School

Mark and Elaine East

Pete Munday

Simon and Katharina Fisher

Richard Fasham

Carl Hingley

Peter Thornton

Andy and Penny Oxley

Dick and Elaine Goodwin

Alan, Gilly, Alex and Hannah Bennett

Pat and Ernie Harpur

Jo, Des, Hugh and Mary Barnett

Trevor and Judith Morris

Phil and Rachel Burt

Birch family - Warren and Jill, Daniel, Evannie, Lydia and Anna

Joe Fairclough

Dr Challoner's Grammar School

Douglas Lanfear

Connie Simpson

Ken Brown

Coniston Fell Race

Jane Webster

St Nazaire Society

Alistair and Linda Baillie

Enid Hill

CNR International

St Luke's Church, Torver

St Andrew's Church, Coniston

Peggy Bailey

Chris Mc Naught

Colin and Wendy Kennedy

Coniston 14

Melbourne ASC

Rumic Foundation Trust

Anna And Mike Dorrington

Riddlesden Methodist Church

Coniston Christian Fellowship

Table of Contents

Foreword by James Beech	19
"A Big Wave, That One!"	21
Small Beginnings	29
The Team	33
Time Was Running Out	63
Floods, Curry, 138 Steps	75
The Waiting Game	89
Relocation, Relocation, Relocation	99
This Is It!	113
Blogs - East to West - 2,500 Nautical Miles	119
We Did It!	299
Hoots of Praise	303

Atlantic Rowing Race start line, La Gomera

Foreword
By James Beech

Reading through my dad's account of our Atlantic adventure it brought back many great memories we shared together. Capturing the true feelings and raw emotions we went through, from the lows of being stuck on para-anchor to the euphoria of arriving in Antigua. This book provides a great insight as to what it's like to spend months on end at sea, incorporating a mix of humour and detail.

Being part of the 'Beech Family', I have always been encouraged to have adventures, being given a sense of independence rather than being wrapped up in cotton wool. Therefore when Dad brought up the idea that he was planning on rowing across the Atlantic, it was almost a natural decision in my mind that it should be something I should challenge myself to do with him. To modify his quote, "It felt good to be in a team with James", it definitely "Felt good to be in a team with my dad".

I would like to direct a personal thank you to my girlfriend, Laura. Thanks for supporting me through the row and still being there when I got home - not a textbook start to a relationship!

"You can never cross the ocean unless you have the courage to lose sight of the shore"
Christopher Columbus (1451-1506)

"A Big Wave, That One!"

Seeking refuge in the cabin, we crawled through the small entrance hatch. We turned the latches which secured the door and made it water tight. We were now in a space no bigger than the size of two domestic bath tubs. We could sit up in the middle without hitting our heads on the cabin ceiling and just about stretch out. However, the cabin tapered towards the stern. To enable us to both lie down at the same time and sleep, we had to settle with our heads at opposite ends of the cabin. It was cramped accommodation for two tall people, but it was our home; our refuge capsule from the turmoil of the ocean.

Before entering the cabin we had spent the best part of 10 minutes setting up and then carefully deploying the para-anchor. This crucial piece of our safety equipment is similar in appearance to a parachute. As we placed it into the sea, the line connecting it to our boat quickly streamed out as we were blown downwind from it. The last few feet of rope zigzagged over the side and disappeared from view.

Then the line pulled tight, opening the parachute and our drift was dramatically halted. 'Beech Boys Atlantic' was now on para-anchor, head to wind, riding the waves and totally at their mercy.

The protection of the cabin meant we were now out of the weather. However, while we could no longer see the waves, a resounding thump, as water crashed against the cabin and the associated shudder of the boat was sufficient to serve notice that they were still there! When a larger wave hit the boat we found ourselves commenting, "A big wave, that one!" This was to be a phrase we would use on a numerous occasions during the row. However, we hardly needed the sound of breaking water over the boat to remind us of their presence. Our bodies were all too aware of every movement the boat made, compelling us to lie down and close our eyes. As 'Beech Boys' pitched and rolled, it was an uncomfortable action and one which quickly stole our appetites from us.

As the sun set, the cabin was now dark apart from the glow of the chartplotter screen and we had both managed to doze off in the cramped and stuffy conditions. The movement of the boat made comfort a difficult commodity to find, despite using soft objects to wedge ourselves in. Every so often a more aggressive wave exploded onto 'Beech Boys' and the rough movement of the boat awoke us from our sleep. It was as though the ocean was shaking us by our shoulders to stop us going back to sleep.

Now we were awake for very different reasons. It was not the turmoil of the sea, but the steady bleep of the alarm emitting from the 'Beech Boys' Automatic Identification System that now had our full attention. Another vessel was in close proximity and our AIS was warning us that we no longer had this part of the ocean to ourselves. It is a fantastic electronic device, able to tell us that another ship is close before we can see it. The AIS brings up a display on the chart-plotter screen giving the name, course and speed of the other ship. We soon called it the SAS, because we could detect vessels before we could see them and it felt as though we had a piece of James Bond's spyware on-board!

The warning bleeps from the AIS forced us to move from our barely tolerable horizontal postures to investigate. We could not easily move together, so we took it in turns to reach a sitting position, holding on to one another for support. Now in the electronic light of the instrument panel we both checked the vessel's details displayed on the chartplotter screen. We could see the track of the other boat was going to bring it worryingly close to our position and decided to call them up on the VHF radio. To our relief, the officer on watch came straight back to us. We had a short conversation explaining that we were on para-anchor and had very limited manoeuvrability. He took details and recorded our position. I could feel perspiration breaking out on my face. The effort of sitting up braced against the cabin bulkhead and the concentration of this relatively straightforward task was a huge challenge which lasted a good five minutes.

Trying not to hit my head in the small cabin as 'Beech Boys' lurched about and having to continuously rule out of my mind any feeling of seasickness took my full attention. As I finished the radio transmission I was grateful to be able to lie down and close my eyes. I just wanted everything to stop moving and give me a chance to regain some feeling of normality. James said he was relieved I had been able to do the radio work, as he wasn't sure he could sit up for that long! If you have ever seen the episode of 'Top Gear' where Jamie Oliver is in the back of a VW campervan trying to make a salad while the Stig drives it around a racing track, you will have some idea of what being in the cabin on para-anchor was like!

"Beech Boys, Beech Boys, Beech Boys. This is Vision of Cornwall, Vision of Cornwall." Our radio came to life again. This time another ocean rowing boat was calling us.

They were close and had heard our conversation with the ship. It was another big effort to use the VHF radio, but it was reassuring to talk to Phil. We could picture him similarly wedged into his cabin making the radio call to us. We signed off and then heard Phil call the same ship we had spoken to and give them his position. James and I lay there and talked about how things might be for 'Vision of Cornwall' and then we were both quiet as we again surrendered to uncomfortable but welcome sleep. It was sleep that separated us from thoughts of feeling seasick and for the moment at least ferried us away from the reminder of the confined space we now occupied and the distance we were from our home and family. Every so often I awoke. If I thought James was awake I asked him how he was. These were always short conversations, but served to reassure us we were not alone!

The sea state was pretty lively and the strong north west wind was edging us towards Africa which wasn't the plan! This was why we had gone on to the para-anchor, as it dramatically reduced the speed we were being blown back to shore. We spent the next two nights and a day on para-anchor waiting for the winds to turn easterly. We were tired and the rest was useful, such as it was. If the ocean was listening to an iPod, it was certainly stuck playing 'Rock Around the Clock'! We both felt out of sorts throughout this time; we didn't want to eat and only nibbled on dry biscuits, crystallised ginger and water.

As we were unable to see land we monitored the wind direction by watching the compass to see if our heading had changed. Being on para-anchor meant our red ensign flag always streamed aft as we were held head to wind. When our compass gave us a westerly heading we knew that our waiting for release from the topsy-turvy world of para-anchor was over. This was the end of our drift and a call for us to return to the oars.

In the early morning before we took the para-anchor in, I fired up the stove to boil some water and made porridge for breakfast. It was going to be my rowing shift first as we resumed progress to Antigua and I felt I wanted some extra 'fuel' for the work that lay ahead. As we hauled in the para-anchor retrieval line we stowed the ropes used to deploy the para-anchor back into their colour-coded bags. After several minutes of heaving on the lines we eventually saw the colourful para-anchor appear like a mysterious monster from the deep in the water ahead of us. We finished our work bringing it back on-board and at last we were good to go.

The wind was blowing from the east and as I resumed our course for Antigua, it was a massive relief to see our flag once again blowing towards the bow of 'Beech Boys'. However, not long into my shift I had to ask James for the bucket.

Another monster from the deep, this time my breakfast, had decided to reappear! Once I had been sick, I felt great! I settled down to the task of rowing, but running through my mind was the thought of how we were going to cope during the next few months at sea if we had more time on para-anchor. How would it be if the wind was stronger and the waves bigger next time? Perhaps that was it and we would now have favourably conditions for the remainder of the voyage. We didn't know and it was no good being overly concerned. We both knew we would help each other through whatever came along. We also knew there was only one way to go - Antigua!

Ocean Reflection:

The slight 'roughing up' we had received from the Atlantic was over. We had visited new territory and we had found our way through it. Ultimately, success in this ocean physical, mental and emotional test was down to the work we had put in beforehand.

Time spent practising underwater escape routines from the cabin, when the boat was upside down, completing a 48 hour row on Coniston Water, sea kayak trips in strong winds and wild seas, the discipline of physical training and the hard work of long hours spent on the project before we ever reached the start line in La Gomera had all served their purpose.

These experiences had equipped us with strength and resolve. A knowledge and understanding of ourselves that brought confidence and the belief that we could go beyond our previous known boundaries. Crucially we knew we were a team. We knew we could trust each other when things were difficult. We knew the other person would stay with it and not give up. We knew we would help each other to achieve our goal.

Small Beginnings

As we continued on our way with the expanse of the ocean horizon surrounding us, my thoughts turned to events from long ago that had led me to this point of being out in the Atlantic with my son. It made me smile as I reasoned that the educational value of an inflatable lilo had perhaps not received the recognition that it deserved. In an effort to put this straight, some attention needs to be given to this important subject. Particularly as that is where the story of 'The Atlantic Job' really has its origins.

Growing up by the sea in Swanage, Dorset, was a big factor in the acquisition of the first family 'sea' going craft - a blue canvas lilo. It had been purchased by my mother for her own relaxation on the beach, but was soon commandeered by my older brother, who saw its potential for waterborne adventures. As Eric was two years older than me, this made a big difference to the activities I could take part in, as my big brother was there to keep an eye on me and in this lilo adventure, my younger sister Gill as well!

It was with great pride that we set off on that summer day in 1967 from the shore of Swanage Bay to navigate the lilo around one of the groynes on the beach. Eric was the captain and sat at the front of the lilo. Gill was positioned amidships and paddled with her hands. I was in the engine room. This technically was not on the lilo, as I held on to the end of it and kicked my legs to propel it through the water. Our cruising range was fairly limited, but the potential for exploration had been established. This important principle, that adventures were out there on the sea, later led to the idea of buying a rowing boat.

The advantage of having an older brother is immense, since it was his ability to bargain with my parents which enabled the purchase of a 'Romany Cat' plastic rowing boat, which was duly named 'Viking' as we broke a bottle of Coke on the bows. We could now head out for distant anchorages around Swanage Bay, often on our own. These journeys seemed fantastic to us and gave us real responsibility for looking after ourselves as we rowed off on numerous cruises of discovery.

My parents were great at letting us get on, trusting us to follow their guidelines, while they watched from a distance and were on hand if needed. On one occasion an easterly wind had picked up while the three of us were out for a row. My mother had noticed the increase in the wind speed and had decided to walk down to the beach to check on us. As waves started to build in size, they created a difficult landing zone for us, on what was now a lee shore surf beach. Aware of the need not to surf down a wave and lose control, we carefully rowed backwards as each wave passed us. This was followed by a sprint for the shore once the wave set had gone through. Gill sat in the bows holding the painter, ready to leap into the shallows at my brother's command. Then the word came from Eric to "Jump out!" Totally committed to her task, Gill neatly stepped over the gunnel and to our total surprise disappeared from view! The water was deeper than any of us had expected, but despite the shock of going underwater, to her credit Gill held onto the painter, swam a few strokes and managed to stand up. 'Viking' was landed safely and we were all relieved to see Mum and have her help to get 'Viking' ashore. This experience was much talked about over the following weeks, but more as a point of how sensible everyone had been than a cause for concern.

The voyages aboard 'Viking' continued and coincided with Mum reading us 'Swallows and Amazons' by Arthur Ransome over the summer holiday. This is a story set on Coniston Water involving two sets of children who go sailing and camping and have their own adventures. We were totally taken with the story and were very keen to 'trade up' to a small sailing boat. After a number of family discussions on the topic of finding a sailing boat, Mum and Dad agreed to look into this if we attended a sailing course. The next spring we were out in Poole Harbour learning to sail. Completing the course enabled us to make the step up to having a Mirror dinghy, which we then raced for a number of years at Swanage Sailing Club.

Other memories of James as a small boy were vivid in my mind. When he was only five years old we had gone rowing together on Coniston Water and he had wanted to have a go at taking the oars in order to row us along. It now made me ponder as I rowed along with James on the Atlantic, how a place I had first heard about in a storybook as a child should turn out to be the very place we first went rowing together.

Coniston Water was also the place where we had completed so much of our training and preparation for this ocean crossing. I found it intriguing as we progressed on our big sea adventure to think back to that first lilo voyage! It had certainly been a beginning, albeit a small but very significant beginning. I wondered what labels might now be attached to a lilo if you were to purchase one - 'Warning: can lead to ocean voyages' or 'Warning: not suitable for crossing the Atlantic'.

Ocean Reflection:

I have learnt to appreciate the value of being given an opportunity. Although seeing an opportunity and deciding to take it is not always easy to do, because often we don't know where it will lead. My experience has been that one opportunity taken can often lead to another one appearing, although not necessarily straight away.

Over the years the significance of stepping up to the mark and giving it your best shot can never be underestimated. There is something to be learnt about oneself whatever the outcome. I found this has helped me to discover my talents, has helped to develop character, expanded my horizons and even moved me on from being a lilo engine room!

It is helpful to remember everyone has to start somewhere. Before we can run a marathon we will need to find out whether we can run a mile! When we can run a mile we can start to believe we can run two. As Theodore Roosevelt said, "Do what you can, with what you have, where you are."

The Team

How had I progressed from the lilo engine room to one half of the first British father and son team to be rowing the Atlantic? It can only be described as the combination of a number of events which over time became an irresistible force! I had followed Francis Chichester's round the world sailing exploits while at primary school. The class I was in had even walked up to Durlston Head, near Swanage, to look down the Channel in case we could see his boat 'Gypsy Moth' arriving back in Plymouth! When I was 10 years old I had been given the book 'Kon-Tiki' by a great aunt and had been fascinated by the story. Similarly, I had read about Ridgeway and Blyth rowing the North Atlantic west to east. They were all achievements which served to inspire and made me think these things were possible.

While at University I had written to Claire Francis asking advice on being part of a Whitbread Round the World crew, but starting a teaching job and meeting Christine, now my wife, before the next race began had meant the timing was all wrong for such a voyage. More recently I had followed news stories of rowers completing the mid-Atlantic east to west route. I was familiar with the challenge of crossing an ocean, but it had until now remained an adventure for someone else. Incredibly the thought that I could complete such a voyage, which had been a fantasy when I was small, was now a startling reality!

I thought back to one particular Sunday when my daughter Lydia had led part of the Church service and asked everyone the question, "What do you dream about doing?" We then had to write down a list of five things. My list included helping to equip other people; retiring early to use my skills in a new situation; leaving a lasting impact; and supporting my family to be the best they can be. Lydia finished her talk with the words, "With God you can". I hadn't written down "Rowing the Atlantic" on my list that day. I had had dreams when younger of wanting to be an astronaut, to be part was rather more positive.

Christine, Lydia and James all wanted to know who I would row with, to which I had no reply. James, who was 17 at the time, said he would go with me! He joked, "Dad, you can't have all the fun!" I hadn't expected that! I knew a key aspect to the row would be how I would get on with my rowing partner. I have always had a strong relationship with James and I had no doubt we could work well together on this project. Over the years we had designed and built his high-rise bunk bed, put up a fence in the garden, gone mountain biking and running together, as well as sea kayaking around the coast of North Wales. I knew James had great leg strength and endurance. When he was 14, he had set a new age group long jump record of over five metres at the National Crusaders Sports, and he could run 400 metres in less than a minute. However the Atlantic Row would be a physically and mentally exacting event and there would be nowhere to hide mid-ocean when the conditions were tough.

I suggested that he took some time to consider the event and the arduous nature of it. James did this over the following weeks and was still confident that he wanted to do it with me. I believed he could. This was going to be about personal motivation and determination. I thought back to the 400 metre relay races I had watched him run the anchor leg for. He had won races for his team from hopeless positions. It felt good to be in a team with James.

For our attempt to be successful we were very aware that our preparations would have to be as thorough as possible in order for both of us to be ready for what lay ahead. The only way this was going to happen was to assemble a top team to be part of 'Beech Boys Atlantic'. So our next move was to tell people our plan and ask for help!

First of all I approached my manager Zena Wooldridge, Director of Sport, when I was at the University campus in Birmingham for meetings. I took the opportunity to let her know what we were planning and to discuss the practicalities of this regarding my job. I had put together an outline proposal and it was a relief to have a positive response from Zena and her boss Geoff Pringle.

Then I wrote to Woodvale Challenge Limited to register our interest in taking part in the Atlantic 2009 race and we sent off our cheque to get the initial information pack.

We knew that raising sponsorship for the row was going to take up a great deal of time, as well as all the other preparations we had to complete. To pull this project together was going to take a huge amount of effort and it had therefore made sense to do it for a worthwhile cause.

A few years ago we had helped our friends Keith and Ally Gibson with a project they initiated when they were working in Senegal, to bring a water pipeline from a nearby town to their local village. The water well in the village ran out of water each morning and villagers were struggling to cope. To raise funds they started a 'Running Well for Water' campaign in which Ally ran the London Marathon. Many other fundraising efforts were organised and I had run the shorter distance of our local Coniston 14, a 14 mile race around Coniston Water. The impact on the lives of the Senegalese villagers when the standpipes providing them with fresh water were installed was immense. Knowing how significant clean water had been to that community had made us decide to approach WaterAid to see if they would be comfortable with us rowing to support their work. To our relief they took us seriously and we went down to the WaterAid office in London to discuss our plans with them. Our aim was to raise enough money to change the lives of 2,000 people in the country of Tanzania by providing them with safe water and sanitation for the rest of their lives.

Rowing 'Beech Boys' out here on the ocean was a fantastic feeling. It was living testimony to the incredible support we had received from so many. We had always been aware that to find the funds to buy a boat, equip it with all the necessary technology and fittings, pay for the race entry fees and our training courses was going to take some doing! James decided he would use money earned from his summer job after he finished his A levels to pay for the RYA courses in navigation and sea survival that we needed to complete. As a family we committed ourselves to cover the travel and accommodation costs. La Gomera, the race start point, and Antigua, the race finish location, are both idyllic holiday destinations and although we were going to be busy working on the boat in La Gomera and in Antigua, cleaning it and getting it ready to be shipped home, we didn't want anyone sponsoring us to think they were paying for us to have a holiday! It had also been easier to explain to people the nature of the project when they knew what we were putting into the row, as some people we talked to tended to see it as a fun thing to do, rather than the endurance challenge it was!

Although we kept thinking of new ideas to raise funds it was difficult not really knowing where it was all going to come from and humbling to see that funds did actually come in. Now as I sat there rowing, the names of all the Nifty Fifty donors were clear to read. They were printed on the inside surface of the boat and surrounded the rowing position. Every day we moved past them as we went about our task of rowing the Atlantic - their names a silent cheer, urging us on. It was a great encouragement to us remembering their association with the project. There was no escaping that start to finish it was a step of faith and these names reminded us of this.

After we had gone public with the plans, we talked to our friend Eric Hoving at Coniston Christian Fellowship, who had set up Bunches internet florist. Eric took an interest in the project and kindly agreed to approach his daughter Dani, who is now the Managing Director. A few weeks later we had a positive response and that initial sponsorship enabled us to commission Woodvale, the race organisers, to build us a fibreglass composite Adkin Pairs boat. It had been a very significant moment and as I looked at the Bunches logo on the boat and the back of the oars it was an ongoing reminder.

It was an amazing experience to keep on track a project that had no reliable income! We were committed to sending Woodvale a cheque for £1,125 each month to cover the £15,000 race entry fee. Amazingly, in spite of all the other costs to pay for the boat and its equipment we always managed to have enough to cover this. Trying to raise sponsorship on the crest of an economic slump was not easy, but God was totally faithful to us and kept us on track.

Significant developments which provided momentum to the project came to us from a number of directions. One day I received a phone call from Jackie Hadwin, the wife of the proprietor of Lakeland Land Rover. She and Jason were interested in having Hadwin's garage name on the boat and kindly sponsored us with assistance from the garage in the form of a vehicle loan to move the boat around when required.

Mike Stather, who worked in the Design and Technology department at John Ruskin School, Coniston when James was a pupil there, offered to help make a stove gimbal system for us. Mike's assistance with all manner of boat fitting out work became invaluable. Norman Murray, my brother-in-law, agreed to teach us how to row! We were planning to visit Christine's family in Northern Ireland and Norman is a member of the Bann Rowing Club in Coleraine. This was particularly helpful as we were just starting to use a rowing machine for our training and we wanted to practise the right technique from the start to avoid developing bad habits which could cause injury.

Christine's workplace, Coniston Corporate UK Ltd, was also very helpful. Colin Reilly, the Accounts Director, introduced us to several companies which enabled us to obtain technical equipment for the row, either free of charge, or at a significant discount. Another help was the generous offer from Saga of an amazing cruise for two, which we used in a fundraising raffle.

James attended the Southampton Boat Show and spoke to as many people as he could about the row. He met Mike Perham on his newly acquired boat in which he was about to sail around the world on a solo voyage. He also had a good conversation with Buffera Headwear which led to them making us 100 bespoke 'Beech Boys Atlantic' buffs free of charge, that we were able to sell to raise money.

Gradually, the project and the large team of people helping us were coming together. A sharper picture was emerging and it contained a lot more people than it did at the start. It reminded us of the scene in 'The Italian Job' when Michael Caine introduces all the members of his task force as they are assembled around the table, each with specialist skills. As we thought about all the people now linked to what we were doing it was immensely encouraging and very exciting. This was just what we needed - a team of greats!

Throughout the months of preparation, Christine and Lydia were always supportive of us even though they would have preferred us to stay on dry land! It was a tougher challenge for them in many respects. Two people they loved were going to be away from them for several months and they were actively helping us to be successful in this separation. We reassured them that we would be able to keep in touch by email and satellite phone, but it is never the same as being physically present and able to share in the day-to-day events of each other's lives. They are very special to have let us pursue our ambition at the cost of their desire for us all to be together.

An important part of the project was going to be the set up of the boat out in La Gomera and both Christine and I thought her friend Pat Menzies would be an excellent support for Christine, James and me. Pat with her sense of humour, unflappable practical nature and ability to gain understanding from Spanish shopkeepers of unusual items we needed for the boat purely by using charades was a huge asset! Could you do a charade to explain that you wanted to buy a rectal thermometer? We were all very appreciative of the terrific support Pat gave us. It was also very kind of her family to let her come out for a week to La Gomera.

Caroline Beckett, another family friend, agreed to collect Christine from the airport when she flew home from the Canaries and to stay in Coniston with her for a few days. This was a big help, as Caroline cooked for Christine when she came home from work in the evenings. Caroline was also going to travel out to Antigua with Christine to provide her with a companion as they awaited our arrival. It was reassuring for James and me to know that such a lovely friend would be with Christine, making sure she relaxed and didn't worry about us.

Further technical support came from a variety of sources:

Ann Kite: a member of staff in the University of Birmingham Sport, was the recipient of our daily blogs and kindly uploaded these on to the Beech Boys' Atlantic web page. Ann was very good at sourcing appropriate photographs to go with the key theme of the story each day.

Alan Phillips: a close friend, who leads Coniston Christian Fellowship and Coniston Crusaders together with his wife Glenda, organised our leaving event 'Beech Boys Bonanza'. Alan also took on the communication logistics of covering for Christine as she was travelling out to Antigua, helped transport us back from the airport and sold more Joe the Swimmers for us than anyone else!

Asker Jeukendrup: a Professor in the School of Sport and Exercise Science in the University of Birmingham, who is at the forefront of sports nutrition for endurance athletes. Asker kindly spent time with us, explaining how to structure our training and nutrition, and generously gave us an introduction to 'PowerBar', who then sponsored us with sports drinks and energy bars.

Jenn Cumming: also on the staff in the School of Sport and Exercise Science in the University of Birmingham, is an expert in sports psychology, and spent time with us discussing our mental preparation for the row and how we would employ different strategies during the crossing to maintain our focus and motivation.

Phil Burns: a member of staff at John Ruskin School, drew circuit diagrams of all the electrical systems on-board so that it was easier to see what would be needed if anything went wrong. We left a set of these drawings with Jason, who wired the boat up for us, in case we ever needed to ring him in the event of an electrical problem. As it turned out, everything worked perfectly, and our circuit diagrams ended up getting a free voyage over the ocean, with no employment required.

Over the past two years there had been so many key points. Each had served to propel us forward. In August 2008, Christine and I were on holiday in Cornwall and had visited the Woodvale Challenge offices to meet the team there and discuss with them the construction of our boat. It was an exciting time as we saw various ocean rowing boats on trailers outside their offices, including EDF Energy, the boat Ben Fogle and James Cracknell had rowed in the 2005 Woodvale Challenge Atlantic crossing. We both felt it moved the project forward and we came away with a provisional completion date for the boat of late December 2008/early January 2009. It was also brought to our attention by the Woodvale team that James at 18 years of age could become the youngest man to row an ocean, although not the youngest person. This honour rests with Rachel Flanders, who at 17 was part of the 2007 Ocean Angels fours team.

In October 2008, during James' half-term, we travelled to London to meet the team at the WaterAid office to talk to them about the row and how we might be able to move forward with the publicity. It also helped us to understand the work that WaterAid is engaged in and we were able to sort out an agreed way of using their logo on our 'Beech Boys Atlantic' materials and website. We also paid a visit to Premier Radio to record an interview that would go out on their Drive Time show. It was our first radio interview and set the scene for future media links.

Later that month Woodvale Challenge organised a training weekend for prospective crews due to take part in the Indian and Atlantic Ocean rowing races of 2009. This was held at Plymouth harbour and gave the opportunity to row in an ocean rowing boat and to listen to a talk by Rachel Smith, who had successfully competed in a previous race. James and I both felt this was a great opportunity to go and find out about a number of topics first hand as well as enabling us to meet other people that would be taking part in the races. We came away with extensive notes on project planning, fundraising, and from all the photos we looked at, a much better impression of what it would be like to be on-board an ocean rowing boat for a couple of months.

In December 2008 (a year before the row was due to start) a team of us spent a busy day in Tesco at Barrow-In-Furness, packing shoppers' bags. It gave us the opportunity to talk to people about what we were planning to do and enabled us to raise just over £500 towards the project. One person we met during this bag pack was Siobhan Winders, a teacher at Pennington C of E Primary School. The school was doing some work on environmental issues and she was interested in our plan to support WaterAid. Over the following months James and I led an assembly at the school and took the boat for the pupils to see. The school kindly supported us with a sponsored walk, again raising valuable funds for the row.

We visited Furness Plastics in January 2009 to see if they would be able to produce adhesive plastic transfers that we could apply to the boat, advertising our sponsors. Bob Ketts, Managing Director, took an interest in our project and the company kindly supported us by providing all the transfers we needed as their sponsorship of the row. Bob is also a member of Barrow Rotary Club and we took the boat later in the spring to show them a presentation about our forthcoming trip.

During January 2009 we visited Sheffield for a training day. A friend of mine, Janet Vickers, who teaches on the Physical Education and Youth Sport degree programme at Sheffield Hallam University, is an international rower and she had arranged a core stability training session for rowers involved in the UK gold team of which she is a member. Janet had thoughtfully invited James and me over to take part, then join them for lunch and a row in some training skulls at Dam Flask reservoir just outside Sheffield. Janet's friend Vicky McDougall spent the afternoon coaching us, and we came away feeling we had a much better idea of what we were doing with our rowing technique. As Janet and Vicky both said to us, with the number of strokes we were going to be making, if we travelled an extra 20 to 30cm on each stroke, it would make a lot of difference after two months at sea!

We decided to organise an evening for our local community to come and hear about the row and where we were in our plans. This was kindly hosted by John Ruskin School as part of their sponsorship of the row, and enabled us to bring people up to speed with the project and its latest developments, which included news of our proposed launch date of Beech Boys Atlantic on Coniston Water on 21st March. The construction work on the boat had fallen behind schedule as the team at Woodvale were busy putting boats together for the inaugural

Indian Ocean race, and we were now due to have 'Beech Boys Atlantic' delivered in March. We wanted to launch it as close to World Water Day as possible.

That evening our local GP, Dr Simon Fisher and his wife Katharina, also a doctor, offered to help put together the extensive medical kit we would need for the row. This was a real boost to us as it was another job which had to be done, and one that we would have struggled with on our own.

At that point, we were also busy selling tickets for a Mediterranean Cruise, which had been kindly donated to us by Saga Holidays. This was a very generous prize and we wanted to draw the raffle at the Launch Day celebrations, so the challenge was to sell as many tickets as we could before 21st March.

This date was rapidly approaching and publicity was out for the launch to take place at Coniston Boating Centre, followed by refreshments and evening entertainment with a Ceilidh. However, our boat was in the final stages of preparation and it was going to be a close run thing getting the boat painted and delivered on time. In the end, Simon Chalk from Woodvale, drove it up himself from the south of England overnight to reach us at the Raymond Priestley Centre for 9am on the launch day. Radio Cumbria planned to make a telephone call to us for a link with their Breakfast Show that morning and it was interesting to hear later that Simon had called into a service station on the motorway, and people tuned into Radio Cumbria had heard about the boat being delivered that morning, only to find that they were sat next to the very boat!

Once 'Beech Boys' was at the Raymond Priestley Centre, we had a busy task getting it set up with a temporary rowing position so that we could row it on the lake at the launch in the afternoon. We also had to apply our sponsors' logos. We were very glad of help from Jason Hadwin and his daughter Jenny, as well as Andy Whitehead, Adam Thickett, Dan Kelly, Steve Wilding and Johan Hoving as time seemed to speed up and the jobs took longer than anticipated! Zena Wooldridge, Director of Sport at the University of Birmingham, then arrived just in time to go and buy some more sandwiches in the village as we had run out of supplies. Zena had agreed to officially launch the boat, and to make a speech at the Boating Centre. So although we were running behind time, we were glad that she had arrived early and was able to help with the launch preparations.

Jason provided a twin-cab Land Rover to tow 'Beech Boys Atlantic' down to the Boating Centre and use as the launch vehicle. We set off in convoy for the village and made our way along the winding road. It was noticeable how long the boat was, and I was very careful driving it down, because while it was insured, it would have been a very costly error to damage the boat at this stage!

At the Boating Centre, a crowd had already begun to assemble, and the gazebo that had been set up to act as a base to sell raffle tickets had plenty of people around it. When I saw the number of people and the limited amount of space we had to manoeuvre the trailer, I decided to ask Jason to reverse the boat onto the slipway as I was feeling rather nervous! It was also one less thing to think about in what was already turning out to be a very busy day. It certainly felt as though all eyes were watching what we were doing and we wanted to make a good impression in terms of managing the boat, which we had never used before and row for the first time in front of a large crowd! At least the weather was calm and we didn't have problems with the boat being blown onto any obstructions.

A reporter from the Westmorland Gazette had agreed to meet us at the launch. She took some photos of James and me, along with the Chairman of the South Lakeland District Council, resplendent in his chains of office. The Launching Ceremony then began.

Zena made a short speech explaining the connection with the University of Birmingham and Coniston Water, and what it meant to the University of Birmingham Sport to have a member of its staff engaged in an Atlantic rowing project. The Reverend Mark East had agreed to bless the boat and prayed for James and me, which meant a great deal to us. This was followed by a short talk from Alan Phillips, leader of Coniston Christian Fellowship. Alan, who does not enjoy water activities, recounted one of the first times he met us when we moved to the area in 1995. Without realising he didn't like water, we had invited him to come rowing with us on the lake!

The champagne corks were popped and sponsors who were present for the boat launch joined us in toasting 'Beech Boys Atlantic'. It was then over to James and me. As Jason carefully reversed the trailer and boat into the lake, we untied the securing ropes to float her off, before stepping on to her for the first time and taking to the oars on the lake. It was great that James took the first strokes, as we wanted people to see that he was quite capable of rowing the boat and it wasn't about him going along with his dad for an easy ride. It was about the two of us working hard together to achieve a common goal.

Launch Day

We were really pleased with that first row. We didn't bump into anything... fall out of the boat... sink... or look silly! The boat looked fantastic, although it still had to be equipped with all the kit that we would need for the crossing. We returned to the slipway and with Jason's help, took 'Beech Boys Atlantic' up to John Ruskin School, where we left her on display outside the main entrance as people came in for refreshments and the evening programme.

During the evening, we enjoyed an excellent Ceilidh and supper. In addition to the Mediterranean Cruise draw, a number of prizes from local businesses had been donated as raffle prizes, and tickets were sold for these during the day. Zena did a great job drawing all the tickets. We weren't sure how we should pick the winning Cruise ticket, but in the end we asked Fiona, a family friend, if her granddaughter would draw it from the barrel, as we felt this would show suitable impartiality! The winning ticket belonged to Christine's employer, Paul Reilly. It was interesting that a local person had won it as tickets had been sold nationally as well as internationally over the previous months!

In the run-up to the boat launch, we had been trying to find somewhere to store the boat. We were really grateful to the Ruskin Museum in Coniston, as they agreed to store it in the recently completed 'Bluebird Wing', which was awaiting the arrival of the restored Bluebird. Donald Campbell had used this on Coniston Water in his World Water Speed record attempt in 1967. So the day after the boat launch, 'Beech Boys Atlantic' moved into its new home!

Tyne-Tees and Border Television had picked up on the story of the row and contacted us to see if they could do some filming of the boat and interview us regarding the project. This began a steady round of contact with Tyne-Tees and Border as they covered our training preparations as well as interviewing us mid-ocean on the satellite phone, and then filming again when we had returned home. The North West Evening Mail, Cumbria Magazine and Radio Cumbria also took an ongoing interest in our story and reported regularly on our progress, both in the build-up to the start, and during the row itself. We were really grateful for this media coverage as it helped to raise the profile of the project.

Although it would have been fantastic if one large sponsor was willing to underwrite the project, we felt from the outset that we wanted to involve as many people as possible, as this would increase awareness of the work of WaterAid. A successful idea we had was the 'Nifty Fifty' scheme, which was aimed at anyone who could raise £50 for the row to have their name rowed across the Atlantic! We also agreed to provide them with a photo of us in the boat, which they could have as a souvenir. This would show the crossing dates and acknowledge their contribution. Gradually, more and more names were added to the Nifty Fifty list, and it was fantastic setting off on the row with the inside of the gunnels displaying the names of these supporters. Several families commented that their children had 'googled' their own name, and been surprised to see in the list of search results a message saying their name was currently being rowed across the Atlantic! It also proved to be a great encouragement to us as we rowed along, looking at the names of people we knew and remembering their association with the project.

During the months following the launch, we took 'Beech Boys Atlantic' down to Coniston Boating Centre to be involved in the Coniston Green Boat Festival and also to the University of Birmingham for the Open Days in June. They were good opportunities to talk to people about the work of WaterAid and what we were aiming to do to support this charity. We also did several local talks, one at Low Bank Ground Outdoor Centre, and one for Kirkstone and Ambleside Rotary Club. Both groups generously supported the project and the Perriwinkles group at Low Bank Ground gave us several excellent connections - Exide Batteries and Blyth Workcats, a commercial boat building company in Canvey Island. Ian Wilding from Exide Batteries arranged for us to have two marine batteries to power our electrical equipment on-board, and Mandy Simmonds arranged for us to store our boat trailer at her workplace Blyth Workcats after we had taken 'Beech Boys Atlantic' to Tilbury Docks for shipping. This saved us driving it all the way back up the M6 and storing it in Coniston until we had to collect the boat after the row.

At short notice we were able to take advantage of a bag packing slot that had become available at Booths supermarket in Ulverston. We quickly assembled a team of bag packers, who helped us raise about £800. James was able to join us for part of that day, after he finished an A level exam at Barrow Sixth Form College.

We wanted to spend some significant time rowing 'Beech Boys' non-stop on Coniston Water. It was a requirement of the race rules that we had logged at least 48 hours rowing time in our boat, of which 12 hours needed to be at night time. So in addition to a number of shorter training sessions, we planned to complete a 24 hour row in late June, and a 48 hour row in early September. It was a good opportunity to try out dehydrated food samples and to get used to the rowing pattern that we intended to use. So on returning from the University Open Days, we drove straight down to the Raymond Priestley Centre, launched the boat and began the 24 hour row at 10.30pm. Johan and Dan helped us get the boat launched and set up. It was the first time we had used the foot-steering system, and it was going to be the first time we would sleep on the boat!

The weather was very calm for the 24 hour row so we didn't learn a lot about how the boat handled in strong winds or rough waves. However it was reassuring to find that the training we had been doing on the rowing machine at home enabled us to easily row our two hour shifts.

As the summer progressed we had positive support from our friend Dave Williamson at Derwent Water Marina, as he agreed to help us source the equipment needed to fit out the boat, which saved us a lot of time. We gradually accumulated more and more boxes of equipment and supplies which had to be stored in the dining room and lounge of our home, as it waited to be fitted to the boat - a task which we would not make any real headway with until late September or early October.

We were conscious that while 'Beech Boys' was a self-righting ocean boat, we wanted to be confident that it would self-right in an emergency, by experiencing firsthand what it would be like to escape from the cabin if for some reason the boat remained upside down and we were trapped inside. So in late August, we launched the boat at the Raymond Priestley Centre, and with Border television cameras filming our trials, we capsized the boat - standing on one gunnel and using ropes attached to the other gunnel, we leaned backwards and pulled. To provide the self-righting capability for 'Beech Boys', 150 litres of water ballast was required. This was placed in plastic containers which were then positioned in the central storage compartments in the hull of the boat. Jo the cook at the Raymond Priestley Centre had been collecting orange squash containers for us to put the water ballast in. These were accumulated over a period of several months and were taken out to La Gomera empty, with a view of filling them with water. In addition to the water being crucial for our self-righting, it also provided a secondary function as an emergency water supply should our watermaker fail.

It took a great deal of effort to get the gunnels vertical, and once the boat did turn over, it very aggressively righted itself, which was pleasing to see. The next step was to re-run this with somebody in the cabin. James went in with a walkie-talkie radio so we could communicate with one another and we repeated the exercise. Despite the weight of James in the cabin, 'Beech Boys' again did a rapid self-righting manoeuvre, after which James emerged from the cabin unscathed and ready to go again.

This time I joined him, and colleagues from the Raymond Priestley Centre worked hard to capsize the boat with both of us inside. Again, the boat righted itself with great ease. Filled with confidence, we moved on to our final test, which was to escape from the cabin while the boat was upside down. The rescue boat was tied up alongside 'Beech Boys' to prevent it self-righting. Adam lent us his underwater video camera so that we could film our exit. We both wore diving masks to assist our exit from the cabin. Having carefully planned the sequence of moves and the direction we were to go in once outside the cabin, we flooded the boat, then opened the cabin door and allowed the lake water in. There was a steady flow of water and as the cabin filled, we both took a final breath before moving into our exit procedure. James was filming so planned to leave the cabin last, and after a few swimming strokes we had both made it safely out of the cabin and onto the water surface. We were then interested to see if we could right the boat with the cabin full of water. So assisting the boat in the same way that you would a capsized sailing dingy, we were able to roll it round and climb back on-board. James made a really good video of our capsize drill, which we then put onto the website and YouTube.

On the wall surrounding the computer desk in our house we posted up a monthly calendar print-out with key events during the row preparation. As early September arrived, the next key event recorded was the 48 hour row on Coniston Water, 31st August to 2nd September. This would help us see how the new XCell oars felt and give us a better indication of the rowing patterns. Our aim was to row alternatively for two hours each in the day and for four hours each at night time to provide a longer sleep for whoever was off duty. The weather for the two days was challenging, with a wet and windy forecast, but we managed to keep our routine going and had also fitted in a good interview with Tyne Tees & Border TV on the second day.

We worked out that 600 lengths of Coniston was the equivalent of rowing the 3,000 miles from La Gomera to Antigua. It was going to be interesting to see how far we could row in 48 hours. As we set off in the late afternoon we had arranged to phone Christine at about 8pm. Our initial row on the lake took us to Peel Island, and then back up the lake to a position just off the Sailing Club from which we could see our house and as we ate our evening meal and the light faded we phoned home and asked Christine if she could see us. As it was now pretty gloomy on the lake, the only way she could see us was if we put our torches on to illuminate our position. We then carried on rowing into the night, but at about 11pm a strong southerly wind halted our progress and we decided to proceed downwind to pick up a buoy and wait for the wind to die down, so that we weren't blown onto the shore, causing damage to the boat. Our handheld GPS showed us that we were doing three knots without even rowing as the wind pushed us steadily along! Compared to the 24 hour row, when it never really got dark, we experienced what it was like to be on the water with no moonlight as the thick cloud blocked out the stars. It was a good opportunity to test our head torches, and thankfully we managed to locate the buoy we aimed to pick up. We both piled into the cabin and listened to the rain and the wind outside of the boat. It gave us an impression of what it would be like in the limited space we had in the cabin if we had to go onto para-anchor on the ocean. However with the small size of the waves on Coniston Water, there was no clue as to how the boat would move around on the bigger Atlantic seas. After a few hours, the wind died down and we were able to continue with our night-time rowing.

After an early breakfast, we made our way back to the Raymond Priestley Centre as we had arranged to meet Tyne-Tees and Border Television to do some filming on the 48 hour row, and we also met Lydia, who was out for a walk, despite the pouring rain! Pat and Ernie Harpur came on-board for a short row with us, and we all managed to fit in, despite limited seating! It was interesting to prove how well our Gill foul weather clothing performed. It was excellent, and despite the continuous rain, kept us completely dry. We had also now experienced the boat's limitations rowing into a headwind, which was painfully slow and at times you could only just see that you were making progress as you looked across to the shoreline. There was a real contrast to each length of the lake that we rowed. Rowing south against the wind always took a lot longer than the wind assisted northward journey. Although rowing on the lake is very different to an open ocean, we began to see how life would be on-board 'Beech Boys'. As we entered into the second night the cloudy conditions continued and it was good experience of rowing in darkness although it was interspersed with glimpses through the clouds to the stars beyond. James even saw a moon bow that night!

At the end of this training row, we felt we had achieved a lot. We knew that establishing a daily routine on-board 'Beech Boys' was a key part to the success of an ocean voyage. So having maintained this for two days was a great confidence boost. It had also helped us to become familiar with the equipment, eating the food we would have on the voyage and coping with living together on a small boat. However it was still only two days and we anticipated being at sea for 60 to 65 days, so it was just a small sample of what was to come and while we had started to experience the difficulties of rowing into strong winds we hadn't yet lost sight of land, or been surrounded by mile upon mile of open ocean! Neither had we been able to test our electrical equipment which was to be fitted later in the month. Despite all our time pressures to get jobs done we were glad we had fitted in the 48 hour row. Mentally it put us in a strong place and would be a solid platform to start the row from, once out in

La Gomera, knowing we could use that routine and work the boat well together, even at night with poor visibility.

In mid-September, we were in Northern Ireland to visit Christine's family for the last time before the row. This afforded us another opportunity to go rowing on the River Bann, with my brother-in-law, James' uncle, Norman Murray. He helped us with technical input into our rowing stroke. Christine's mum was on a mission to help us increase our body weight as we had planned to each gain a stone in body weight before the race started on the 6th December. We were grateful for all the 'wee buns' and extra portions of food provided at meal times. Even if we didn't gain a lot of weight while we were there, we certainly had a lot of extra weight in the car on the way home with all the food supplies that she sent us back with.

WaterAid had put together a really good feature about the 'Beech Boys Atlantic' row in their 'On Tap' magazine. They also had a good article featuring us on their website. These articles were very important, as individuals and companies supporting us could then check out our link with WaterAid and see where the funds raised would be channelled.

We appreciated the encouragement brought to us from so many people, who went out of their way to help. Andy Adamson with his expertise in pilates provided practical support on posture and exercise. Claire Farrow gave us guidance on publicity and her boys, Daniel and Jonah, even wrote to Blue Peter to tell them what we were doing. Julie

Flanagan, ran the Great North Run to raise funds for us. Chris McNaught organised a fundraising lunch and this led us to have a connection with her neighbour, Eric de la Torre MBE. Eric is one of the Commandos that took part in Operation Chariot in the Second World War. Their story was retold by Jeremy Clarkson in the BBC programme, 'The Greatest Raid of all Time'. The St. Nazaire Society, established to preserve the memory of Operation Chariot also support WaterAid and this stirred his interest in our row for the charity.

To remember each of these stories was inspirational. They all served to keep us connected with all the hard work that had gone into firstly getting us onto the start line and now out onto the ocean. It was motivating to reflect on how we had progressed and the people and circumstances that had enabled each step to be made. We did not want to let anyone down after all they had done to help us. We wanted to do the best we could for WaterAid and that meant not giving up. Keeping our goals for each day clearly in mind was key to success. Although no sooner was one situation sorted, the next was emerging from below the horizon and appearing on our 'project radar'. As my dad would have said, "There is always something!"

Ocean Reflection:

Throughout this time we found the encouragement of having such superb support served to develop momentum and drive, propelling us forward. We knew from the outset that on our own we were very limited in terms of our own technical knowledge. The close interest in what we were doing from so many experts with their practical skills, the presence of positive people, each with their own particular talent kindly 'donated' to the project was invaluable. They were all fundamental to the project. If we had a 'Beech Boys' board of directors, they all had a seat on it!

Time Was Running Out

The summer had been a busy time of researching equipment that we needed to install on the boat. Calculating how much power we needed to run it, how reliable it was and could we afford it? In addition we had to keep on training, talking to possible sponsors about the project and putting a plan and timetable together in order to complete all the jobs. It was a very tight schedule.

Our friend Jason Hadwin, proprietor of Lakeland Land Rover, Torver, had kindly offered to help wire up the electrical equipment we would have on-board. As we had sat down with Jason at his home one evening to talk about this, it was evident the wiring would take longer than we had anticipated. We knew Jason would do his best to finish it in the time available, but it was a worry for us all.

We were planning to visit the Southampton Boat Show on 16th September 2009 to buy our navigation equipment, EPIRBS, battery monitors, marine wire/cables and battery switches. Jason was unable to start the work until he had the equipment and then it was a case of fitting it in after his day job. By this stage James had finished his A levels and summer job, so was available to become Jason's assistant, and hopefully learn how everything worked, which would be crucial if anything needed fixing when at sea.

Our September programme was as follows:

Southampton Boat Show - purchase equipment. This was a full-on day of meeting up with suppliers. Marine Electronic Services and DBS both gave us good deals on the navigation aids we needed. Mactra Marine provided excellent advice on setting up our watermaker, while Barden Batteries gave helpful tips on setting up our solar panels and battery monitors.

RYA Courses - we had a number of compulsory courses to complete in order to be able to take part in the row. We had to pass them first time, no pressure! We arrived for the first morning of our eight-day set of courses and as we walked into the training room, several of the other crews were there in their pairs, and it felt a bit like the scene from the film 'Top Gun', when all the crews are at the Top Gun academy, trying to work each other out! However, it turned out to be a great time of getting to know other crews and when we arrived in La Gomera a few months later we quickly felt part of the event, as we were reunited with those we had met on these courses.

As we travelled to the course each day from my mum's in Highcliffe we would listen to the radio, and one day heard an item about Buzz Lightyear becoming the longest serving member of the International Space Station! This gave us an idea to take a bath swimming toy I had been given as a fun leaving gift from colleagues on the Executive Committee of the Association of Heads of Outdoor Education Centres as the first bath toy to swim an ocean! One night as we had a drink at the pub with Joe and Chris, the crew of 'HCL Workforce

1', they suggested we contacted the toy importers and tell them about our 'swim the Atlantic' idea to see if they were interested in sponsoring us. It was a good move and they kindly donated 150 bath tub swimmers for us to sell or give away. This also transformed us into the support boat for our bath toy, now called 'Joe the Swimmer'!

The night before the final Ocean Yachtmaster exam, James and I walked down onto the beach at Highcliffe and looked out into the English Channel. We both picked up a stone from the beach and then walked to the edge of the shore before throwing them into the sea. We had a moment to pray together, committing the coming months of preparation to Jesus and asking for strength and skill to keep on top of the tasks that lay ahead. It was also a special moment to give thanks for all that had been achieved.

Wiring of the boat - installing all the electrical equipment, the watermaker, solar panels etc. This was a BIG job! We knew how crucial this was. Once we were at sea we did not want to be fixing problems. So having Jason do this work for us was brilliant. He was incredibly thorough and we were able to trust him completely. That was exactly what we needed at this pressurised time.

Keep on training! - If days were particularly busy then training time had been before work, or late at night. Everything was full-on and training was put on the back burner some days, as the list of jobs to be completed grew longer. We were fortunate to have sponsorship from Lakes Leisure in Ulverston. They supported us with gym membership which enabled us to row together from time to time rather than on our own at home. A superb display of ocean facts across the walls in the gym was accompanied by a 'Row the Ocean' competition, with a boat being moved along a line marking the 3,000 miles as members of the gym clocked up miles on the rowing machines.

Go to work! - During all the preparations, I was still working full-time for the University of Birmingham. Fortunately James had finished his A levels and was able to work on the boat, otherwise we would have failed to keep up with the daily schedule of tasks.

Looking back now, it was a massive task. We had calendar sheets up on the wall at home with timetabling for all the jobs. We had day-to-day A4 sheets up next to the boat, charting what needed to be done each day and these were numbered to clearly show how many days we had left before the boat needed to be at Tilbury Dock, London on 21st October for shipping out in a container to La Gomera.

Besides Jason, we also had the help of Mike Stather, who had generously offered his time to build a gimbal for our gas stove. This offer of help was then extended to all manner of boat fitting out tasks, to which Mike directed his attention and expertise. James was very busy at this point in the preparations, as he helped Mike during the days and Jason during the evenings! Mike was superb in his accuracy and attention to detail, fitting the solar panels, rowing positions, bilge pump, cabin vents and improving with his own additions other pieces of equipment, for example new buggy axles and spacers for rudder fittings to reduce cabin noise as the rudder moved on its mountings during the voyage.

It is true to say that without Jason, Mike and Jason's father-in-law Don, we would not have had the boat ready for shipping and probably would not have made it to the start line. They were all fantastic and we can never thank them enough for their commitment to help us. Ironically the item of kit Mike had initially volunteered to build for us, the cooker gimbal, was not finished when 'Beech Boys' was driven down to Tilbury due to all the other jobs Mike had worked on! So we took the gimbal system out with us in our luggage to La Gomera in November once Mike had had the time to produce it without any other boat building distractions.

Besides fitting the boat out, a variety of other important tasks had also been underway. We had decided to produce our own breakfasts for the row, so Christine had purchased a vacuum packing machine to create watertight packets of cereal; 150 grams of Ready brek and 50 grams of dried milk powder were added together and vacuum packed, to create one breakfast portion. The plan for the row was that hot water could be added along with sultanas and golden syrup to give an adequate breakfast each morning. It sounds a simple task to make up these packages, but Ready brek is a very fine product and the smaller particles kept being sucked too far up the packet, preventing a proper seal from being formed. So producing 180 breakfasts took a long time!

Overall the vacuum packer was a useful purchase, as Christine was able to seal a large supply of her mum's renowned Christmas cake which brightened up many of our days during the row.

Our final day of work on 'Beech Boys' before taking her down to Tilbury was 20th October. The oar supports made by colleagues at the University of Birmingham, School of Manufacturing & Mechanical Engineering were bolted on. Carl and Peter who work on the formula student racing car programme had done a great job on these for us and saved Mike the time in building them. Carl had kindly sourced specialised plastics and stainless steel nuts and bolts for us which again saved us a great deal of time. Richard Fasham from the same department had made various backing plates for us to use when bolting equipment on to the boat and supplied us with the hand drill we would take with us as part of our tool kit.

As that day had rolled on we came to the final job of packing everything that would need to go on the boat out to La Gomera into one of Jason's Land Rovers, which he provided for us to tow the boat down to Tilbury. We ended up doing this at the Land Rover garage in Torver in their main working bay, as we could get the boat and the vehicle into one place undercover, as the evening's forecast was for rain. A team of helpers from Coniston Christian Fellowship helped tidy up all the leftover bits and pieces from the fitting out work, as well as transport all the food supplies and other equipment from our home to the garage for the onward journey to Tilbury.

As we looked at 'Beech Boys' that evening we knew everything that could have been done to get her ready had been finished. It all looked absolutely brilliant. Our only qualm was that the first time we would see her afloat fully fitted would now be in La Gomera and the expertise of our support team would only be available by phone. However this was tempered with the knowledge that the work had been done to a very high standard by people we trusted completely. In the end we lost no sleep over this and once in La Gomera the quality of the work stood out a mile, as everything worked perfectly! It was great to report back to Mike and Jason on this knowing they were eager to hear that everything was operational. F.A.B. Virgil..!

Another friend from church, Johan Hoving, volunteered to help with the driving. So a final team of Jason, his son Joe, Christine, Johan, James and I worked on the packing, applying sponsors' logos and cleaning the boat before finally finishing at 11.30pm. Jason drove 'Beech Boys' out of the work bay and parked in front of the petrol pumps. James then had the idea of getting a photo of him filling up the boat with fuel! A number of people have now seen this photo and asked where the engine was, to which we have had to explain it was just a joke and we were rowing, not motoring, across the ocean!

We needed to have 'Beech Boys' at Tilbury for 11am the next morning, so Johan and I planned to take it in turns to drive through the night. First of all food, showers and strong coffee were required so we drove home for this before eventually setting off at 1.00am with Christine waving us off from the deserted street. As I looked in the mirror I could see James surrounded by packages of equipment. “Are you feeling a bit boxed-in, James?!” I asked. We all had a laugh and felt a terrific sense of excitement at what lay ahead. All the graft of the last two months had brought us to this point. We had a beautiful boat which we felt very secure with. The sense of satisfaction at what had been achieved was tremendous. The ‘dream team’ that had helped were much talked about as we drove down through the night and we thanked God for their support.

Throughout the journey to Tilbury, James stayed awake to talk to whoever was driving which was a terrific effort on his part. At one point when I had been sleeping, I awoke to James and Johan laughing. They were playing a game in which you worked through the alphabet using each letter to describe something that you thought was “a bit rubbish!”, Johan was explaining why “X-men cake was a bit rubbish!” This was a particularly funny moment, particularly as he had the same letter ‘X’ in an earlier game where you had to explain why something beginning with that letter was “Really great!” On that occasion everything about “X-men cake” had been great rather than rubbish!

We had a steady journey through to Tilbury. As we drove along the dockside Johan suggested we stopped to get a photo of ‘Beech Boys’ in front of a container ship which was on the other side of the dock. Although it wasn't the ship 'Beech Boys' would be shipped out on, it made a great picture, with the name of the shipping company 'Grimaldi Lines' clearly painted on the container ship's hull and WaterAid clearly visible on ours.

Grimaldi Lines

We had arranged to meet Nicola Bourne from WaterAid at the dock so she could see 'Beech Boys' before being loaded into the container. It was good to be able to do this as it helped us remember what we were hoping to achieve for WaterAid through the row. It was a great photo opportunity too with the WaterAid logos on the side of the boat and the background of the dock, reminding us we were on the next stage of a big adventure. A number of other rowing boats were also at the dockside awaiting shipment. It was a strange thought, as we watched the crane lift 'Beech Boys' off the road trailer and on to the cradle that would go into the container, that the next time we would see her again would be in the sunshine of La Gomera and not the rain of Tilbury.

Before driving back to Coniston we dropped the trailer off at Blyth Workcats on Canvey Island. This extended into a tour of the boatyard and a very welcome tea break before heading back up the M6!

As we arrived home it was peculiar to see such an empty lounge and dining room. The boxes were all gone. Only the 'jobs to do' lists still up on the walls were testimony to the massive amount of work we had all accomplished. However, while there was a cause for celebration there was still more to be done on the fundraising and personal preparation for the row and that soon occupied our thoughts and filled our lives during the next few weeks. It would not be long until 19th November and our flights out to Tenerife and the ferry to La Gomera!

Ocean Reflection:

Undoubtedly the daily 'jobs to do' sheets that were pinned up on the walls of the work area around 'Beech Boys' were crucial to having 'Beech Boys' ready. At the top of each piece of paper was printed the number of days we had left, which helped us to keep our focus and maintain a sense of urgency to keep on top of the work. We detailed the work to be done each day on the relevant paper which gave us the satisfaction of crossing the job off the list when it was finished! A great way of seeing we were one step closer to our goal.

These lists made the difference between keeping the project on target and finding we were overwhelmed. It would have been all too easy to get things out of sequence, or find we had forgotten to do something.

The reality of the BIG team was it had made a massive task manageable. To reach the start line was an achievement in its own right. The BIG team had put us in a position which on our own we would have been unlikely to attain.

Floods, Curry, 138 Steps

Our good friends Alan and Glenda Phillips prepared a local send-off for us in the form of 'Beech Boys Bonanza!' Their daughter Gemma, and her husband Mark have both represented Great Britain in Athletics, and Alan had the idea of asking them to run with some of their GB team mates in a relay over 3,000 metres - to correspond to the 3,000 miles we would row. Local people were challenged to form a team to see if they could beat the GB athletes over this distance. The event was called 'The Unfair Games' to identify the fact that it is unfair how a lot of people in the world do not have access to clean water. While we all failed to get close to the GB runners, teams did succeed in raising funds for the row through sponsorship.

By the end of 'Beech Boys Bonanza', this amount along with proceeds from the Trash and Treasure stall and sales of refreshments at the Beach Cafe, where my daughter Lydia was singing, over £1,000 was raised for the row. We were able to say farewell to a large number of people, give a final press interview for the Evening Mail and Westmorland Gazette and publicise again the fundraising work we were doing for WaterAid. James and I had our WaterAid T-shirts on and asked the GB runners to sign these for us, as we intended to take these with us on the row. It was a wonderful send-off and Alan asked everyone to give us three cheers! So at the end of 'Beech Boys Bonanza', we certainly felt ready to go, with the backing of the local community.

My last few days at work at the Raymond Priestley Centre focussed on tidying up loose ends and checking with staff that they were familiar with the Centre's action plan and the work they would be doing. Steve Wilding, our senior instructor, would lead the team while I was away and his experience and understanding of the Centre's programmes would be ideal for keeping the Centre on an even keel. The staff presented me with a framed picture, an old chart of the Atlantic ocean, which was really kind and a suitable reminder of what lay ahead.

The autumn had been particularly wet in the Lake District and the day we were set to drive to Manchester airport was exceptionally so. Water was flowing steadily down the road outside our home and when we received a phone call from Vicky Pollitt at Tyne Tees & Border to say she couldn't get through the floods to Coniston to do an interview with us for the regional news, we started to wonder how we would get on driving out of Cumbria later that day. After a call to Zena, we had permission to use the Centre's Land Rover and this enabled us to meet Vicky, who then drove close behind us through the flooded sections of road back as far as Greenodd. The Ship Inn generously opened up just for us and Vicky was able to do her interview inside the pub. After this it was back through the floods to Coniston for a final pack-up of our personal luggage before driving to Manchester where we were going to meet up with Lydia. The extra time used to do the interview had put us behind schedule and it was a busy final hour of packing up before we set off again in the Land

Rover. The countryside was transformed with the floods and we kept saying "Hey! Look at that!" as we gazed out wide-eyed at the impact the floods were having. We couldn't help but see the irony of not being able to get out of Cumbria to take part in an ocean rowing event due to floods!

Johan had offered his services as a driver again and so we changed vehicles at Greenodd and he took us in his car to Manchester. Part way down the M6 I suddenly realised that in our rush to get packed up, I had only brought the charging unit for the power drill! We had bought a cheap drill set which if necessary we were happy to leave behind in La Gomera. However the power pack on its own was no use, but at least I had remembered at this point. So Johan was able to take the power pack back with him. Fortunately in the hectic departure that was the only thing we forgot and Richard's hand drill proved itself to be entirely adequate for the jobs we had to do in La Gomera.

We had planned to stay overnight in the Travelodge at Manchester airport, and Lydia got the train from Sheffield University to meet us so we could all go out for a meal. Christine had booked a table at Asian Fusion in Chorlton-cum-Hardy, a superb curry restaurant we had visited several times before and we thought this would be a fun family meal out. Christine told the waiters that we were about to row the Atlantic and to give us some extra big portions - so James and I were then challenged to try and eat the ridiculous amounts of curry they brought to the table! At the end of the meal the difficult task of saying goodbye to Lydia had arrived. Big hugs and kisses followed, knowing we would not see each other for a few months.

Andrew Phillips, Alan and Glenda's son, met us and drove Lydia to Stockport, where she stayed the night with him and his wife Sarah. This worked well, since she hadn't wanted to get the train back to Sheffield on her own late at night, having said goodbye. Unfortunately Lydia's course exams were due in February, which was when we thought we would complete the row in Antigua, so she would miss our arrival at the finish line. We all found this difficult as we wanted to have the end as a family event celebrating the efforts everyone had put in to make it possible.

Johan then took us to the Travelodge and our last farewells were made to him. Christine, James and I turned in for the night with a mixture of emotions. Sad to have left Lydia, excited about what lay ahead, relieved that we had come to the end of our preparations in the UK and had reached the end of this part of the project.

The next morning the strange collection of boat parts in our hand luggage took a little bit of explaining as we went through airport security. However, once we mentioned Woodvale Challenge's Atlantic Row, the staff knew what we were doing since two of Manchester Airport's firemen Dean and Neil were taking part with their boat 'Spirit of Manchester Airport'. So we were soon through and into the departure lounge.

In Tenerife we travelled by ferry from Los Cristianos to La Gomera. It was good to meet with James Ketchell at the ferry port. He had been on the same RYA navigation course as us back in September.

It was pleasant to be in the warm sunshine after the rain of Cumbria. Once in La Gomera we made our way to our accommodation. En route we walked by the compound where all the rowing boats were being stored. It was great to see 'Beech Boys' waiting for us and to meet the other rowers. La Gomera side of operations was now underway!

Our accommodation was a flat in a lovely location looking down on to the harbour, although it did take a bit of walking - the route was uphill with a final run of 138 steps to get into the flat! However, it gave a good daily leg workout and helped keep our fitness levels ticking over.

That evening we met Pat at the ferry port. Christine knew her from her Salford University days. We wanted to have a top support system for Christine, so Pat was there to lend a hand with the practical jobs of getting 'Beech Boys' packed up and ready for launching, as well as being good company for Christine. To make settling in easy that first evening, we went out for a pizza and had a fun time catching up and planning what needed to be done over the coming days. Pat was a huge hit with Joe the Swimmer!

The next day James and I were keen to get going to sort out the boat's equipment and prepare 'Beech Boys' for the scrutinising check. Christine and Pat were busy putting 90 bags together with all the food supplies we had brought out and to fill up all the water bottles with the 150 litres of water ballast the boat needed for its self-righting capacity.

James checking out the cabin

We soon got to know the crews in the boats next to us in the compound - Paul and Jim in 'The Reason Why', and Rob and Stu in 'Ocean Summit'. The atmosphere in the boat compound was always friendly and crews were willing to help each other tackle any odd problems they had, which was great. However, before long it was evident that we all had a mutual problem to deal with. Each boat had to have a specific number of flares and these had all been packed into a separate shipping container because they were classed as dangerous cargo.

Unfortunately the paperwork for the flares had not satisfied the Spanish authorities and were not permitted to be released from customs. This proved to be an ongoing problem for Woodvale Challenge, the race organisers, who now had to source new flares for all the boat crews.

The boat compound was a real sun trap, as it faced south and had cliffs behind. So working there was hot! We drank large volumes of water to keep hydrated, but rarely visited the loo! The combination of the heat and standing up all day to work on the boat made my ankles swell, so when we returned to the flat each night, it was definitely time to put my feet up! The highlight of that first week was having lunch each day with Christine and Pat in the shade at a small beach a few minutes walk from the compound. There was always a breeze there, which helped to cool us down. There was also a small bar which served very cold beer. The first time we joined the girls, they had already bought a beer for themselves. We noticed that they had been given a very nice plate of olives. However, when we ordered our beers, no olives were produced! We concluded that the waiter was obviously more taken with their charming personalities than our chunky rowing physiques!

After the scrutinising we had a couple of jobs to sort out. The tap water Pat and Christine had filled the water bottles with was not deemed to be a good idea, just in case the containers were not clean enough and the water became undrinkable after months at sea. Consequently we had to buy a new set of water containers (150 litres) from the nearby marina shop.

This gave us plenty of water to clean the boat with, but then we had to find a place to dispose of the 30 water containers we no longer had a use for. So we decided each time we walked back to our apartment from the boat we would take some with us and put them into waste bins on the way. This reminded us of the scene from the film 'The Italian Job' where electronic disrupters are placed in dustbins to put the local traffic lights out of action. We joked about the effect our containers would have on the local Christmas lights!

At the end of our first week in La Gomera, Pat returned home to her family in Scotland, and my mum (James' grandma) came out to help during the second week. Christine travelled over to Tenerife with Pat to the airport and then waited for Grandma to arrive. They stayed in a hotel overnight in Los Cristianos and came over the next day on the ferry to La Gomera.

Our boat had by then passed scrutineering and we were waiting our turn for the boat to be lifted into the marina. We wanted Grandma and Christine to see the boat being lifted in and the timings worked out perfectly. As we were taking the boat round to the lifting point, they arrived off the ferry and saw the boat being lifted with James on-board. There was a final touching up of the anti-fouling paint and the boat was lowered into the water. James and I were then able to row the boat round to a suitable berth in the marina.

Lift into Harbour La Gomera

During the next week, the remaining jobs on the boat involved checking the fore-aft trim of the boat, greasing all the bearings for the buggy seats, programming the GPS chart plotter with the waypoints we intended to use, and running the watermaker. Our first watermaker check was a little worrying as a small part kept falling off the piston rod into the bottom of the battery box. After some careful checking of the assembly diagrams and advice over the phone from Jim MacDonald at Mactra Marine, we sorted the problem. A simple rubber boot fitting had been put on the wrong way when we had been checking the manual operation, and once refitted, it worked perfectly.

As the week went on, the problem of the flares continued to dominate everyone's thinking and in the end was a distraction from what was happening on the weather front. For the race to start, the port authorities insisted that there had to be five consecutive days of good weather to enable all the crews to get safely away and out of their international waters. Although we had been enjoying some fine weather, conditions were changing and the Azores High (an important weather system that would block low pressure systems from coming across the mid-Atlantic) had broken down and a series of low pressure systems were forecast to come across from America. During one of our morning race meetings with the Woodvale race team officials, it was announced that the weather changes were likely to result in a postponement of the race start date of 6th December. The various scheduled briefings continued to go ahead, and fun events were planned by Woodvale in the form of a fancy dress evening and a Paella evening for the crews and their families.

On the 3rd December, it was my 50th birthday and Christine had packed various cards and gifts. We had a champagne breakfast before going up to the Parador Hotel to meet Doctors Simon and Katharina Fisher, our doctors in Coniston, who were on holiday in La Gomera, and were planning to wave us off.

We also had a chance to test the boats in a short five mile race called the 'La Gomera Cup' organised by Woodvale. This was held on 6th December, when the race should have started. It took us out of the harbour in a dry run of what would be the proper start line and then around the two lap circuit using 'Aurora' and 'Ocean Planet', the two race support yachts, as the markers to row around. It was a fun event and we felt it gave us some good feedback on our boat set-up, and we decided to change the foot steering set-up to reduce its stiffness. It also meant that Christine and Grandma were at least able to see 'Beech Boys' in action and the spectacle of all the boats out on the water at the same time, since they would miss the official race start due to the postponement. Their flights home had been booked for 8th December just in case there had been a delay to the start, but we had thought that the worst case scenario would be a 24 hour delay. So it was a strange feeling for James and me to wave them off on their journey home, rather than them waving us off at the start of the row. At this point we thought the race would start the next day (9th December), so we had given them all the cash, clothes and anything else we did not plan to take across the ocean.

When they got to the airport they said goodbye to each other. It was only later that we discovered that Grandma's plane to Bournemouth had been delayed and she had to sit on it for an extra few hours until it could go. Christine's flight to Manchester was then delayed until the evening. Rob from 'Ocean Summit' arrived at the airport with his parents, and gave Christine the heart sinking news that the race had been postponed further and would not start the next day. Christine's immediate thought was that we had no money, no accommodation sorted and no extra clothes! So she gave Rob her debit card so that we could get cash out, but she did not know how we would be able to sort out extra accommodation since she had organised all that with the agency. In fact, only that week she had emailed Liz at Casas Canarias to extend our accommodation from the 6th to the 8th.

So it was with a sinking heart that she went through the airport security and sat down in a bit of a daze on a random seat in the departure lounge. She had spotted a lady a few seats down from her doing a crossword, but was too busy praying about the situation to notice much more of what was going on around her. Twenty minutes later, the lady leant across and asked Christine if she was Mrs Beech, since she had noticed BEECH marked on her holdall. She went on to explain that she was Liz from Casas Canarias! She knew that the row had been delayed, and had wondered that day if Mrs Beech might need extra accommodation for her husband and son. Christine confirmed this was the case and Liz rang her work colleague to sort this out and arranged for our use of the flat we had been staying in to be extended at a discount until the start of the row! Thoughtfully Liz sent James a text to let us know this. A grateful answer to prayer, as we were thinking that we would be sleeping on the boat every night. We knew there would be plenty of this ahead of us once the row began. This guardian angel even shared a beer with Christine before they went their separate ways!

It was a difficult time waiting in La Gomera on a 24 hour standby. We continued to do some tinkering jobs on the boat to keep ourselves occupied and attended the morning nine o'clock meetings to keep up with developments in the weather and a possible new race start date. It was a tense time for all the crews, as supporting family had now travelled home and many people were finding it difficult with tight budgets that had not reckoned on a longer stay in La Gomera. There were also work implications for many rowers if the delay was prolonged as they had arranged specific time periods to be away from work.

Woodvale arranged a number of activities, including taking a photo of all the crews as viewed from the masthead of the support yacht 'Aurora' while she was in the marina. We all crammed onto the foredeck of 'Aurora' while the photographer was winched to the top of the mast! The result was a great souvenir photo.

The Fishers continued with their holiday in La Gomera and we met for coffee a few times to keep them up to date with what was going on. They came back on two occasions to see us off, but neither of these turned out to be race starts, and in the end they had to return home and we were left on our own.

As the postponement was prolonged further, we wondered how to explain to our landlady that we would like to rent the flat for longer. Christine had taken our Spanish phrase book so with only our very limited Spanish we decided a better option was to converse using 'pictionary'! We drew the days of the week onto a piece of paper, with a picture of a bed next to each date. There was then a tick and a cross with a question mark after it to indicate which days we would be able to stay there. The lady found it very amusing, however we had managed to communicate what we needed.

Ole Elmer from team 'Boogie Woogie' decided it would be fun to cheer everyone up with a party, which he kindly organised at the Parador Hotel. We felt a bit awkward about our attire at this respectable hotel, as we only had a couple of pairs of shorts and T-shirts left on the island, since Christine had taken the rest of our kit home. However the other rowers were in the same position and the hotel was very welcoming to everybody and made it a memorable evening. Ole was very generous in paying for everybody and it certainly served to cheer us all up and provide a welcome distraction from waiting for the race to start.

Ocean Reflection:

Although it was difficult to adjust to the ongoing delay to the start date of the row we knew it was important to realign our goals. We decided to see the delay as a gift of extra time in which to make further checks and fine tune our preparations. This gave us something purposeful to do each day and helped to keep our mind on what we were there for. We made it our aim to know we had not left anything unchecked. We did not want to find ourselves on the ocean regretting we had not used this extra preparation to its best effect.

The Waiting Game

As the race was scheduled to start on 6th December 2009, we decided we should begin to write our blog entries. Although we weren't able to begin the row, supporters were following events and we wanted to keep everyone up to speed with developments as they unfolded. This chapter is made up of the blogs written from the internet cafe situated in the main square of La Gomera adjacent to the Town Hall. The background noise was always made up of the sound of electronic bells on various game machines and the aroma of waffles and coffee never seemed to leave the air.

6th December 2009

Beech Boys' Log

Today was scheduled to be the race start. However with problems arising from the delay to get all the flares for the race boats through customs, we are in La Gomera until Wednesday 9th December. Currently the race is due to start then.

For those of you old enough to remember 'Wacky Races', it all feels like the start of one of their events! Everyone is ready to go with engines running, but Dick Dastardly and Muttley have chained the cars together and no one can start! All being well, Dastardly and Muttley will soon reverse into the lamp post, snap the chain and we will be off!

As an interlude to the wait for the flares to arrive, a small race was planned for this afternoon in the bay outside La Gomera's harbour. For families having to travel home, who will now miss the real start, this at least provided a good impression of what things will look like on Wednesday. 'QBE' were the 2009 La Gomera Cup champions, perhaps an indication of things to come when the real race starts? 'Beech Boys' finished in midfield, with a much better second lap after a few steering issues on lap one. A top speed of 4.9 knots was pleasing, although that was only for a short spell as we pushed for the finish line. It was certainly good to be out on the water and to be doing some proper rowing!

On-board 'Beech Boys Atlantic', we are feeling well prepared. We have spun out some of the jobs to provide something to do each day. It has been great to have people coming along to see us in the marina. We had a surprise visit from a lady who comes from Birmingham, but now works on La Gomera. She had a press cutting in her pocket from the Birmingham Evening Mail about us, which she had kept since June! We had been on the University campus with ´Beech Boys´ for the Open Days and the paper had featured our story. It was interesting to see how far clips from the Birmingham press travel and great to meet up with support from the Midlands!

As you can imagine, Joe the Swimmer has been ´wound up´ by the delays. Swimming lengths of the bathroom sink is not what Joe has come out for and he is a bit like a coiled spring at the moment! Anyway, he will have his chance to strike out for Antigua fairly shortly.

The next update from BBA should be from the water. We will be in touch...

8th December 2009

Beech Boys' Log

Good news! The flares have arrived - hurray!

Bad news! The weather forecast for the next few days is not good - too windy to allow time for all the fleet to clear safely the island of El Hierro and progress into the open ocean - booo!

The pantomime start to this update may fit the seasonal entertainment at home in the UK better than it does the rowers here in La Gomera. The event has to start safely, as there is only one chance to get the fleet away. Any problems and the local port authority will not permit things to proceed further. In fact it is a 10,000 euro fine if you try and get away while no one is looking! The Salvamento Maritimo - the local coastguard, will come out to tow you back in and impound your boat! So for the time being we all await the right five day weather window.

It feels strange now that nearly all the support crews made up of rowers' family and friends have returned home. As a result of the various delays it does feel like the film 'Groundhog Day' at the moment. We get up, go to the marina, work on the boat, talk to the same people around us at the harbour and look out to sea, but we just can't break away to get out there!

Anyway, the view at the moment is that we may not be underway until sometime between Saturday 12th December and Wednesday 16th December. So we have made our plan of how we will usefully use these days to do some further preparation before the strong winds arrive. This will involve testing the para-anchor set up, improving our steering system controls and developing shark wrestling skills! We joke not! James was in the water helping to fit the rudder pin when someone passing by commented there was a shark! We took this as the usual joke people make and we carried on. Although no relative of Jaws, we found out later that in fact a small shark had been seen in the marina that afternoon! Anyway it is good to see James doing his own stunts and not using the shark cage.

9th December 2009

<u>Beech Boys' Log</u>

Yesterday evening Christine's flight home was delayed, so after seeing my mum Corinne off on her flight, she had a long wait at the airport. Our friend Caroline met Christine at Manchester Airport and she was able to stay the night with her, although they didn't arrive at Caroline's until 3.30am!

Besides re-organising our domestic arrangements we have been working on improvements to the foot steering which we have still not quite got as we would like. It has been very hot working on the boat today, sun but little wind, which makes it all the harder to believe strong winds are on the way!

10th December 2009

Beech Boys' Log

This morning has been spent in weather and ocean routing meetings. The weather is set against the race starting just yet, so the whole fleet is on standby for the time being.

This afternoon we have been afloat using the time to practise using the para-anchor. This is an important piece of equipment and looks like a parachute. It is deployed into the sea and the boat drifts downwind away from the para-anchor until the 100 metre rode line goes tight. The wind blowing against the boat then keeps this line tight and the resistance of the water inside the para-anchor drastically reduces the amount the boat is blown downwind. It also makes the boat sit more comfortably for the occupants, as it stays head to wind and the waves pass around the bow of the boat. It does require some careful organisation, as there is also a retrieval line which collapses the para-anchor and enables it to be brought back on-board. So there is over 200 metres of rope and the para-anchor to bring back on-board onto a small section of the boat when conditions improve!

11th December 2009

Beech Boys' Log

Watching the weather is the order of the day. The collapse of the Azores high pressure is allowing low pressure systems to track further south than normal, providing strong headwinds which would stop an ocean rowing boat in its tracks. The projection for the next few days is for the southerly winds to continue. As soon as the northeast winds set in, we can get away safely from La Gomera. The islands funnel this wind into what is known as the 'acceleration zone'. Getting into this along with help from the Canarias current gives a fast route over the 55 nautical miles to El Hierro, the most southerly of the Canary Islands. After this, boats will follow their chosen route to Antigua. The shortest route, the rhumb line, is not necessarily the fastest. Going further south, although longer in terms of miles, provides scope to pick up better following winds and thus provide a payback on the extra miles rowed south. In the current situation of the winds blowing in the opposite direction to any observed trends from the past five years it does make for a more complicated decision, as staying North on the rhumb line could result in catching the bottom edge of low pressure systems and finding the headwind too strong to row against and therefore result in time on the para-anchor. Going south to catch better winds may not work either, as they are currently proving unreliable, hence the delay to the race. We have been plotting several options on our charts today with a view to being able to switch plans once clear of El Hierro when we can assess conditions out on the ocean.

We were really interested to receive news from Caroline who is staying with Christine in Coniston at the moment. She woke up from a dream with a strong sense that there would be "No more delays!" So along with many others we are praying for the right weather to get everyone away safely as soon as possible.

That is it for now. We must track down Joe the Swimmer before he runs up any more bills on the credit card. He is a bit of a shopaholic!

12th and 13th December 2009

Beech Boys' Log

STOP PRESS: Weather routing meeting scheduled for 15th December to decide whether we'll go on 20th December, or if the race will be postponed until late December.

Saturday 12th December - After overnight rain it was a cloudy day today. We have been sailing on the support yacht 'Aurora' with a four hour trip out into the 'acceleration zone' - the strip of water between La Gomera and Tenerife. Fortunately 'Aurora' is a BT Challenger yacht, so with a heavy steel construction she provided a stable platform, in what was a pretty lumpy sea. We headed south along the west side of La Gomera, so we could see the stretch of water separating La Gomera from El Hierro, before returning to port. Although the wind at about 25 knots was stronger than the port authorities will allow us to start in, it was a worthwhile exercise providing a good close up of the possible sea conditions we could be starting in.

We have picked up emails from so many people congratulating us on getting this far. One from the Bowles family was particularly encouraging, saying “Keep the blog going even if you don’t row anywhere, you’ve achieved so much!” The messages have been terrific and a real boost while we’re waiting. Thanks.

News update on Joe the Swimmer! Joe is about to undertake an incredibly technical challenge and we have had to apply ourselves as a team to look at how best to tackle some of the difficulties that await him in the water. Obviously keeping joints working is essential. We have gone off the idea of traditional cod liver oil tablets, rather fearful there could be a backlash towards Joe from some of the ocean’s inhabitants once they realise he has eaten some of their ‘fish relatives’. So we have been experimenting with a high silicon content spray supplement, which is administered in very carefully controlled doses. This isn’t something that should be tried at home! We have James, a highly skilled operative, who knows exactly what to do, and readers need to appreciate we are at the cutting edge of science on this. Quite possibly there may be spin-offs, or spray-offs, akin to the NASA space programme after this event! Just a quick note to say we managed to get the credit card back from Joe, he’d only bought a new swimming hat, so no expensive purchases thankfully!

Sunday 13th December - We ran the watermaker again today. Now that it is all set up and already been used it needs to be run every two to three days to stop any micro-organisms growing inside the system. To do this we row outside of the marina to get the cleanest sea water we can and run it for 10 to 15 minutes. The watermaker draws sea water through a pre-filter before forcing it through a membrane to remove the salt. The pressure involved is high at 800psi (to give an idea, your car tyres are perhaps between 20 to 30psi at normal load). It therefore requires a powerful pump and certainly on our boat the watermaker is the most power hungry piece of equipment we have, and the most essential. It will be operating for about four hours a day to give us 25 litres of water. This has to supply both of us for all our needs every day.

How would you get on with 12.5 litres a day? Lots of people around the world have not much more, perhaps less and not drinkable, which thankfully our water is. This is of course what the project is aiming to help with as we provide funds to WaterAid to make a difference in 2,000 people's lives.

Ocean Reflection:

The benefit of having access to email became evident as we made our daily visit to the internet cafe. It connected us to our family, friends and supporters, enabling us to let others know what was happening which was important. However, we found that telling others our news, usually in a humorous way, was a release valve of sorts. It helped us to share the situation we were in and it brought a fresh perspective to it.

It can be easy to create ever bigger mountains out of life's molehills. We wanted to keep a positive outlook to avoid finding we had introduced an automatic default setting of seeing everything as being set against us. We were not seeking a denial of the problems we faced, but we found being positive assisted us to find solutions and kept us strong as a team.

The support we received from emails throughout the voyage was terrific. We enjoyed the mental challenge of thinking up different storylines for the daily blog. We also valued the tangible lift we received each day as we read out loud the emails Christine had forwarded to us. Reading the messages out loud seemed to help us to 'picture' the writer and the encouragement of their words being audible on-board 'Beech Boys' was a gigantic psychological boost.

Relocation, Relocation, Relocation

The weather had remained unsettled and in the end it didn't seem to be a surprise to hear that all the weather experts agreed there was no indication of any immediate change developing in the weather patterns to provide for a race start before Christmas.

As we walked to the meeting to hear about the official race restart date, it was raining, windy, warm and humid! At the meeting the long range forecast showed the current low pressure moving through followed by the start of a high pressure area re-establishing itself, but the wind, still from the south was in the wrong direction for us! The meeting decided that the restart date following this postponement would be the 29th December 2009, with teams needing to be in La Gomera from 27th December for boat scrutinising and obviously to prepare mentally for the start. We moved into our La Gomera exit plan.

To recap on the reason for the postponement, there had not been a sustained period of good weather to allow all the boats time to row south from La Gomera to pick up easterly winds to make the row across to Antigua. Instead strong southerly winds had been making any attempt to row south from La Gomera a non starter. At 22 degrees north, there have been easterly winds. This is the latitude we need to row down to from the start line, but there has been no way of reaching these favourable winds by rowing boat! Hence the postponed start to the race. This weather was unusual and certainly not what is normally experienced at this time of year and therefore completely unforeseen. Certainly the weather of the last ten days would probably have left teams in a vulnerable position having made little headway and been worn down by three or four day stints on the para-anchor.

Over the previous few days we had made up our minds that if the race was postponed until after Christmas we would travel home. The flat we had been living in had to be vacated as the extension we had been given was now up. If we were staying in La Gomera longer we would have to move onto 'Beech Boys'. Leaving that day would mean arriving in Coniston at 3am on 16th December but we would benefit from seeing family and friends. It would also enable me to get into work through to Christmas and for us to celebrate Christmas at home. We would be able to continue with some light training over this time to maintain fitness levels.

Before we left La Gomera we made a final check of 'Beech Boys'. The boat was ready for the crossing and was looking good to go! We arranged with Leo Rosette, one of the rowers staying on La Gomera, to run the watermaker every few days for us and passed on a couple of carrier bags of food to Alex and Luke from 'Yorkshire Challenger'. We couldn't take this home and they were staying out longer than us, although still hoping to return home for Christmas.

As we said our goodbyes and left La Gomera on the ferry it was with a real sense of leaving behind unfinished business.

It wasn't over. This wasn't the way we planned to leave La Gomera. We weren't travelling in the right direction and we weren't on the right boat. We would not be at sea for Christmas. However, as Arnie once said, "I'll be back!" We knew we would be back to finish the job. The Atlantic Job wasn't over yet.

It was odd travelling into Manchester wearing our summer kit. All we had in La Gomera were a couple of T-shirts each, some shorts and Crocs, so arriving from 23 degrees to 3 degrees wearing these items was refreshing to say the least! Fortunately Christine had some warmer clothes for us to put on as she met us at the airport with our friend Alan Phillips, who had kindly driven her to the airport to collect us.

Over the next two weeks we knew we had to keep a firm grip on our intentions, so we didn't lose the momentum we had worked so hard to achieve. We were also aware that waiting and waiting for the start had been wearing on us and we decided to use the time off the island to provide refreshment and a spur to get on with the job once we were back on the 27th December.

As you can imagine the change of our location for Christmas had some serious repercussions on Christmas arrangements. For weeks Santa's reindeer had been on a top secret rowing camp to enable them to do a stint on the oars mid-ocean during Christmas Eve. We even had special handles made so they could grip the oars! After such careful planning it was a pity to have to pull the plug on this. However, on a brighter note we thought everyone else was much more likely to have their presents delivered on time, without the detour to 'Beech Boys'!

We suspected the volume of presents intended for Joe the swimmer may prove to be a hindrance. He had been dropping hints about getting designer swimming costumes for Christmas! We had been working hard to keep the weight of items going on-board 'Beech Boys' as light as possible. So it would have been difficult to either find the space for such a large influx of extra kit, or get excited about rowing it over the ocean! Anyway Joe would now spend Christmas with us in Coniston which would help us to monitor what went back to La Gomera!

We sent a message in our blog for everyone in Vicky McDougall's rowing group in Sheffield and for the rowers in the Munrow Sports Centre at the University of Birmingham. They were starting their indoor row to cover the same distance as us, but the postponement of the race meant we were unable to start our row at the same time. We did appreciate their enthusiasm for the project and said we would do our best to catch up!

Extreme weather encounters continued to be a theme for Beech Boys. We had the Cumbria Floods when we left Coniston in November, winds from the wrong direction in La Gomera and now snow and ice in Cumbria! However, it all looked most seasonal in Coniston with a good layer of snow everywhere. It was a winter wonderland! I went to work in the week running up to Christmas and was able to join in with the staff

Christmas meal which was fun. As we spent time in Coniston a number of people did a double take, not expecting to see us there. So we had to recount the story of the race postponement more than once or twice.

So what do ocean rowers do in this ‘waiting to go’ time? We decided to avoid any activities that may cause injury! So having both decided not to ski - James on Helvellyn with Johan and me cross-country skiing into work each day - we elected for the safer pursuits of James tobogganing in the nearby field and me cycling to work on snowy paths! This wasn’t the exercise I thought I would have been taking in the build up to Christmas. James and Lydia also had time to build an igloo in the garden!

James and I did some training on the rowing machine and some core stability work. There was also the important task of eating! Not normally difficult to do at Christmas, but we wanted to keep up our weight knowing that ocean rowers typically lose weight during the time they are at sea. This is because it is incredibly difficult to eat the number of calories being used each day. So we had a target of putting on a stone before the race start to provide a fat reserve that would disappear during the row and stop us arriving looking like stick men! Although we had been working on the weight gain from September, now we were at home that still needed to continue, particularly for James, who loses any weight he gains very quickly! “Another mince pie anyone?” “Yes please, I’ll have three!” Payback time would start all too soon, as we would begin to eat our dehydrated rations once underway on ‘Beech Boys’!

In the meantime, we really enjoyed Christmas at home. Delivering some Christmas post, attending the village Christingle Service which Lydia sang at, celebrating Christmas with friends from church on Christmas morning, having Christmas lunch and opening presents together were all brilliant to do and we would have missed them by being at sea. While we were soon to be away for the re-start we savoured this time before the hard work of rowing to Antigua really began. We can't say much about our Christmas presents as we had left these behind in the boat as surprises to open on the voyage!

It is fair to say our minds were struggling not to be elsewhere. In a strange way it would have been easy to stay at home, rather than say goodbye again. It was a big effort to push on and get back out there. We also knew we were going back with no support crew, no one to help cover the simple everyday jobs of sorting out meals and taking an interest in what we were doing. Our support network would be via the less personal means of email and telephone. At least these existed. We often thought of earlier voyages where communications were far more difficult, or even non-existent, as people ventured off in an even more isolated fashion!

After a bit of work on the internet we sorted our travel arrangements to return to La Gomera on Boxing Day. It started to look like we were in a 'Top Gear' challenge, trying to beat Jeremy Clarkson to La Gomera! The return journey involved flying from Leeds/Bradford airport into Gran Canaria, getting a taxi to our hotel, finding the port entrance, getting a few hours sleep in the hotel and then off on the ferry to Tenerife, another taxi, another ferry and then we would be there on La Gomera! Friends Erica, Ian and Faye Caswell and Erica's mum Sheila all travelled over to see us at the airport and wish us well, which was very kind of them. After a short round of conversation, it was that moment when we had to say a final goodbye. We all kissed and hugged and were reminded to "Take care, look after each other and have a safe and successful crossing to Antigua".

It was a strange feeling going back on our own. A bit like going back to school after the summer holidays! We knew it would probably be OK once we were out there, it was just that we weren't quite 'there' yet! James and I walked away from Christine and Lydia and I pretended to trip up. It was one of my silly family jokes that normally brought a smile, which I thought might lighten the moment. However, one of the handles on the plastic carrier bag I was carrying broke and I then had to improvise, tying the two handles together into one! It all held together and no further repairs to our luggage were required.

On arrival in Gran Canaria we took a taxi to our hotel and after checking in went for a stroll to see where the ferry would go from the next morning. It was midnight and we ordered a pizza from the takeaway at the end of our street, which we ate as we walked to the harbour. It was an early boat and we wanted to be sure we knew the way. We were back at the hotel at 1.30am and then got up at 6.30am to walk to the ferry. The agreed return time for crews was 3.30pm on 27th December. As long as we didn't miss any connections we would be fine.

Our ferry to Tenerife brought us into the north of the island and we then had to get to Los Cristianos in the south for the ferry to La Gomera. As we queued for tickets at Los Cristianos for the final ferry journey we met up with several other rowers and it started to feel as though we were being spliced back in again to the loose ends we had left behind.

Over the following 48 hours we knew there would be a final check of the boats before crews set off on the 29th December and that it would be a very busy time checking through everything and making our final preparations to get ourselves 'in the zone'! As we walked from the ferry terminal to the marina we saw Simon from Woodvale and quickly learned that the race wouldn't be starting on the 29th after all! After pushing ourselves to get back on time it now felt strangely peaceful again. Suddenly we had lots of time to do everything and get ourselves together for the row. We were also back to not knowing when we would go and we were playing the accommodation extension game again! Fortunately Christine was able to work on this for us and extended our stay as the delays continued. As we had crossed to Tenerife we could feel the Atlantic swell of some five to six metres and this was the cause of the slippage from starting on 29th

December. Eventually the start date was moved back to 4th January, as the swell would create problems with boats being carried east onto the African coast. It was starting to become a more serious issue now. If we didn't get away soon perhaps the race would have to be cancelled rather than postponed.

It was a time of concern for us, as well as the other crews and the Woodvale Race organisers. James and I spent some time looking back over all the things that we had been involved with. The answers to prayers, the encouragement brought to us by our friends and the fact that we were out there with a boat ready to start the row were all powerful reminders of God's faithfulness to us. As I had once heard it described, it is good to keep a 'God Factor' checklist. When uncertainties crop up it serves as a real anchor, something that steadies the ship at a time when waves of doubt are building. In our current situation these were all very useful analogies!

Over Christmas the weather had been poor in La Gomera with heavy rain and strong winds. Waves broke over the marina sea wall, so they were a reasonable size! Our boat was fine, although we discovered the roof hatch in the main cabin was leaking, so we had to dry the mattress out and make repairs to the seal. This was all fixed thanks to James' hard work. While he worked on the hatch I checked and repacked all the boat's equipment and we were both happy with how 'Beech Boys' was set up. Will and Tom from 'Heritage Explorer' had stayed in La Gomera over Christmas and made up a Top Trumps game based on all the boats in the event. It was brilliant and a unique reminder of all the teams taking part in the race.

Before Christmas, walking to our accommodation had involved a lot of steps and was a good workout for the legs. Now we were only a short walk from the marina. We no longer had the grand view of the harbour, but it was very convenient. However, the main drawback with our new flat only became apparent at night time. We both found we were being woken up by the sound of mosquitoes buzzing around our heads. Each night we ended up having to hunt them down in order to get back to sleep. James' approach was to swat them with his pillow! Judging by the little squished insect marks on the walls and ceiling this had clearly been the approach adopted by others before us! One night we were both disturbed at the same time. Switching on the light always meant our eyes took a moment to adjust and in this time the mosquitoes seemed to 'go to ground' and become difficult to find. So on this occasion as I jumped out of bed and switched on the light I shielded my eyes from the light by putting my hand up to my forehead and looked around the room to see where they were. James burst out laughing, as it looked as though I was scanning the horizon for invading hoards! I joined in the laughing and for the rest of the time on La Gomera we got the giggles remembering the search for the mosquitoes!

Preparations for New Year's Eve were in full swing in the main square just next to our flat. It was going to be a noisy night of celebrations! The various crews met up at the Blue Marlin pub for a drink and then there was the countdown of the local clock as midnight approached. A local tradition is to eat a grape on each chime. After wishing each other well and watching Pete Van Ketts perform a dance as he waved a lit hand flare, we retreated to the flat and put in some ear plugs!

As the next few days passed the 4th January continued to look good for a start date. As part of the procedure for departing we had to hand in our passports to get the official paperwork signed off in order to be able to leave Spain. It all started to feel like this was going to be it. We were really going this time! Woodvale's strap line is, 'Woodvale Challenge - The World's Toughest Rowing Races'. For a long time it had seemed to us we were in one of the world's toughest waiting events! This was no longer the case and we were about to take part as father and son in one of the world's toughest rowing races. We were excited and calm all at the same time. Everything we had been working towards, all the help and support we had received was now coming together for this one moment - the race start 1.30pm on 4th January 2010.

On 2nd January the swell was down to two to three metres with a favourable northerly wind direction, as high pressure became more established again. The high pressure was pushing the lows north and providing the favourable northerly wind we needed to help get us south into the trade winds. An ocean rowing boat is stopped in its tracks if there is more than 15 knots of headwind. You can keep rowing, but the circular 'puddles' created by the rowing stroke don't fall behind the stern of the boat. A clear indication the boat is not moving forward and you are just marking time. Once the wind is strong enough to stop you, it doesn't take much more of an increase in the wind strength to actually start pushing you back over the ocean you have already rowed. You can keep rowing, but your efforts are no longer taking you in the direction you wanted to go! So having the right conditions is crucial in order to clear the Canaries and the African coast.

The night of the 3rd January and the pizzeria next to the Blue Marlin was our destination for our last meal out. After a number of previous visits we had tested a good number of the pizzas and James had established his favourite as salami and garlic. I went for spaghetti carbonara. We wondered what we would have as our first meal once we were in Antigua! We decided to have a final haircut before we started, so once back at the flat we got the scissors out and tried to remember what our hairdresser Sue usually did. The results weren't too bad and the next couple of days we had a little phrase that made us laugh, "Hey! Nice haircut!"

Ocean Reflection:

Would we ever begin to row the Atlantic? This question went unanswered for far longer than anyone could have predicted. The boat was ready, we were ready, everyone wanted us to start, but a further factor outside of our control was the key to being able to start. Very simply, it was the need for a period of settled weather. Ultimately we were part of an event and Woodvale together with the Spanish Port Authorities had to make that call regarding the weather conditions.

To start and just 'go for it' would have made us feel good, up until the point we were asking for a tow back in! Everything could have been lost because of a reckless and impatient moment. The pressure to get started was immense. The consequences of a wrong call would be painfully severe.

Throughout the pressure of this uncertain time we could do almost nothing to change our circumstances. However, we could decide upon our attitude. This would influence how we conducted ourselves, the decisions we made and how we eventually approached the row. Therefore we made it our aim to retain an optimism outlook that we would start. We also sought to maintain our enthusiasm for the row. Finally we had to be patient.

Timing is often crucial. As it turned out once we did start, a settled weather pattern, that would have enabled us to begin with a favourable five day forecast never appeared again.

"Difficulties mastered are opportunities won."

Winston Churchill

This Is It!

Surprisingly we slept well and were then up early to get to the local supermarket to buy some green oranges and bananas, cake and some tomatoes to take with us. I cooked up a fresh batch of chicken and pasta which we put into plastic bags for our evening meal that night. It was then time to check out of the apartment and get down to the marina. Robert and Caroline on-board the yacht 'Aragorn' had invited any rowers that wanted bacon butties to come over to their boat. We took them up on their kind offer and Robert gave us a quick update on the weather for the next few days which still looked good.

The last hour ashore seemed to pass very quickly. We wanted to get round the other teams and wish them well. We took photos of Alex and Luke by their boat 'Yorkshire Challenger' and they took ones of us by 'Beech Boys'. All the crews had longer together in the run up to this race than would normally happen and there was a great sense of comradeship between us all. Running round to say goodbye to everyone was a good warm-up to going afloat. Then we had to go! We manoeuvred 'Beech Boys' out of her berth and rowed carefully out of the marina to join the fleet of boats now assembled across the start line.

We decided to take a gentle approach to the start and enjoyed the moment, as spectators waved and cheered from the quayside and a local commercial ship sounded its foghorn. We took photos of other boats and as we rowed along the coast 'Aragorn' resplendent with bunting in the rigging came across to wish us well and take some photos. Simon in the Woodvale RIB motored past and we waved and said, "See you in Antigua!"

This was it, we were off. We had prayed earlier that morning for the day ahead. We hadn't forgotten anything and we had time to soak up the atmosphere. It was now all about establishing the on-board routine and adapting to life at sea and surviving on fewer hours of sleep than we had ever done before!

4th January 2010

Beech Boys' Blog

Sent from La Gomera before we went afloat

After more than two years of preparation, here we are on race day. Weather is looking favourable for the first week of the row. Atmosphere on 'Beech Boys' is buoyant!

A BIG "thank you" to everyone who has helped us along the way - we are only here because of that support. We will aim to do you proud, as we find our way to Antigua!

Final systems check on 'Beech Boys' today went something like this:
Satellite phone? Go!
GPS? Go!
Watermaker? Go!

Life jackets? Go!
VHF and comms? Go!
Solar panels? Go!
Batteries? Go!
Oars? Go!
Food? Go!
Alarm clocks? Go!
Seat padding? Go!
Loo bucket? Go!
Joe the swimmer? Go!
Beech Boys Atlantic are GO! GO! GO!

Every day worldwide 4,000 children die from illnesses caused by poor water and sanitation. That is more than die from AIDS, malaria and measles combined. Knowing our efforts to support such valuable work would be an on-going motivation as we rowed the ocean.

PS At the weigh-in James was 82kg, I was 90 kg. The weight gain effort had been successful!

<u>Ship's Log</u>

After final goodbyes to other crews and photos of us on-board just before we cast off, it was then out to the start line and jockeying for position with the other boats before departing La Gomera at 13.30. The start horn was given from the support yacht 'Aurora' and we were underway. Hooters blared from the local commercial dredger and 'Beech Boys' was last to cross the start line as we soaked in the atmosphere and took photos of the start. A good northerly breeze helped us on our way for the first hour. The Woodvale RIB with Simon and his family and Manero from the Blue Marlin motored by and waved us off. 'Aragorn' with rigging full of bunting has a short conversation with us and told us to "Keep safe" as they took photos and video. The wind turned against us and we saw 'Boogie Woogie' and 'Dream Maker' behind us and 'Rames Dames' closer inshore all engaged in the same battle - to make progress into the wind. James and I rowed together until 9pm and then began to row in shifts with the start of a four hour rowing pattern overnight. Our first meal on-board was chicken pasta which I had made that morning in the flat before we left. We thought it would be good to have fresh food and not have to set up the cooker that first night.

As night set in, we could see the navigation lights of the rowing boats around us and 'Ocean Planet', one of the support yachts. We were on our own. The waves were all over the place as we rowed through our first night and began to acclimatise to life on-board. The moonlight helped us to pick out the waves and steer accordingly. We felt confident as we set off leaving La Gomera behind. Knowing that we had completed a 48 hour row on Coniston Water was a great boost and put us in a positive mental place.

Ocean Reflection:

While all the preparations were taking place we always had people around. In our normal lives we were used to having lots of people around us. Now we were two people alone, surrounded by an ocean desert. So once we started the row, we again appreciated that everything we looked at on 'Beech Boys' had a story attached to it. Each story was linked to a person or family and served to remind us of what had gone before, what had taken us out onto the Atlantic ocean.

This personal attachment to our surroundings helped to provide a positive mental fix on what our mission and purpose was. Through the good times and the hard times these stories were a spur to us, reminding us that behind us there was an invisible crowd of people still cheering us on, keen to see us complete what we had set out to do.

Beech Boys off La Gomera

Blogs - East to West - 2,500 Nautical Miles

Here, the story of the Atlantic Job is told via the blogs written throughout the voyage. These were aimed at telling our story in a humorous fashion. Extracts taken from the Ship's Log help to provide insight into how we felt and cover details missed from the blog, which was written each afternoon, whereas the Ship's Log was written at the end of each day.

5th January 2010

Ship's Log

The sea was very lumpy with waves from different directions. But at least the wind was from the north, and blowing 15 to 20 knots. We had top speeds of 5.1 and 6 knots as we surfed. Neither of us was particularly hungry. We had been getting used to the waves, but being inside the cabin was not particularly comfortable. As the waves died down during the afternoon, life on-board became more straightforward. I spotted some dolphins, which made a brief appearance, also a ship's lifebuoy. Overall the conditions have helped us make good mileage. We were pleased with the performance of the solar panels - the batteries have all recharged really well.

6th January 2010

Beech Boys' Blog

Written and sent from Ann Kite, University of Birmingham Sport. Norman and James not yet in 'Blog Mode'!

We at UBSport are eagerly awaiting our first blog from Norman and James at sea, but in the meantime thought we'd send you a graphical depiction of their progress.

At the time of typing, the boys have been 2 days, 2 hours, 31 minutes and 22 seconds at sea.

All the crews are travelling predominantly south, so while they are covering good distance, they aren't making direct ground to the finish.

Bit of a statistic for you fact fans: assuming all teams make it to the finish, they will have rowed the equivalent of halfway to the moon!

<u>Ship's Log</u>

The wind has been from the northwest, again 15 to 20 knots. There has been a two metre swell with wind-blown waves moving across, so it has been hard to make progress to the south. We overheard 'Vision of Cornwall' and 'Heritage Explorer' on the VHF radio. They are in a similar position to us, getting blown to the east. At 5pm, we decided to go onto the para-anchor. We were both tired. We phoned home on the satellite phone. Christine said that it was great to hear James' voice this morning when he rang. It had been difficult in Coniston to just watch a green dot on the website, and not be able to find out how we were feeling.

Johan who was providing us with weather updates had called in to see Christine and Lydia and was there when we phoned so we got a useful weather update from him. We sent a text to Simon at Woodvale to let him know that we were on para-anchor. We tried to sleep but the boat was being rocked around in quite a lively fashion by the waves, and it was not easy to rest.

7th January 2010

<u>Ship's Log</u>

Overnight there had been some big waves crashing onto the boat. We checked the GPS chartplotter and were pleased to see that 'Beech Boys' had held its position well on the para-anchor. Our AIS bleeped at us to alert us that a ship was in close proximity, and we spoke to the bridge crew on-board 'Renate A' to check whether they had us on their navigation instruments. Phil from 'Vision of Cornwall' heard us make the broadcast and we had a brief chat to him on the radio after he also spoke to 'Renate A' to check they had noted their position too. Later that night, another vessel, 'RBL Tank France' also registered on our AIS and we checked with them also to ensure they had our position. We spent the day on para-anchor, and tried to maintain our on-board routine by running the watermaker. The movement of the boat was particularly uncomfortable. We both felt out of sorts and James was struggling with a sore tummy. The only way we could stay comfortable was to remain flat, lying down in the cabin. At 5pm, just as we went to bring in the para-anchor, the sea got up again so we decided to stay put and spent another night on para-anchor, with the aim to head southeast the next day with the forecasted wind change.

8th January 2010

Ship's Log

We kept checking our position and the wind direction overnight, with neither of us getting much sleep. It looked as though there was a northeasterly wind, and at first light we were heading off to waypoint 2. James took domperidone tablets for his tummy, and we tried to establish a normal eating pattern. I had porridge and apple for breakfast, James was on plain biscuits. We got the stove going, and made a cup of tea. We filled our flasks with hot water so that later on we could use this to make up the dehydrated meals, which would save having to light the stove again later. I was briefly sick and then felt much better.

During the course of the day several cargo vessels were spotted. A spectacular sight was seeing the tall ship, 'Alexander D Hombolt', come onto the horizon. It passed fairly close to us, but was heading in a more southerly direction. We carried on through to 9pm on our two hour rowing shifts. James was still not feeling 100% so we tied everything down on deck and let the boat drift on the easterly wind. We both spent the night in the cabin, but didn't really get a lot of sleep. Our senses were finely tuned. The movement of the rudder on its fittings echoed in the sound box of the cabin. In fact every sound on the ocean seemed amplified, as we were still getting used to all the noises the boat made!

9th January 2010

Beech Boys' Blog

News sent from Christine to Ann Kite to go out on the blog: 'When James rang this morning he was feeling much better, and they have managed to get into a routine of daily rowing shifts, cooking, resting, etc - so they are in good spirits. They have encountered a few large boats on the shipping lanes, and it is reassuring to know that the AIS system which detects them is working, and they were able to avoid them.

They apologise that they haven't been in touch through their blog, but getting the laptop going and typing was too much of an effort over the last few days as they have been tossed about in the cabin! They hope to start up again with this soon. They want to thank everyone for all the support they have been receiving, which is such an encouragement to them.

To let you into a secret - I think they are beginning to regret taking Joe the Swimmer with them since he has been swimming towards Africa, and thus pulling the boat with him - he fancied visiting some friends there while he was in the area! He owes them big time now!'

Ship's Log

The AIS pinged at 6am, so I got out of the cabin to investigate and keep a look out, while James read the GPS chartplotter. We saw the ship's lights and it passed fairly close to us at

6.50am, so we got up and started the cooker, making flasks of hot water. We both had porridge and tea for breakfast. The winds were getting lighter, and we got a text from Simon at Woodvale to say that Roger Haines was close by in 'Dream It Do It', but we couldn't see him!

We rowed our shift pattern through the day and enjoyed seeing a Storm Petrel circle the boat. A big tanker came up on the AIS this morning; it passed clear of us but we were amazed by how many boats we were seeing! James was feeling stronger and felt more able to eat, which was good. Spoke to Christine on the satellite phone at 10.30am. She said she had emailed lots of messages to us, which we were excited about. Up to that point neither of us had felt able to sit in the cabin to type on the computer. During the afternoon two small sharks passed close to the boat with their fins very noticeable on the surface. They didn't stay for long!

The light winds continued throughout the day and the evening and we decided to continue with our night time rowing. The sunset was quite amazing with the sea streaked with silver, blue and orange. It was very calm with only an occasional wave and a slight swell before the wind died out completely. The stars were wonderful overnight. Once we had the boat set up on our compass course, we took our line from the stars and found these more comfortable to look at than the digital compass display. For my 50th birthday Christine had bought me all the James Bond audio books, so before we left home, James had uploaded all these onto his iPod, so that night we both enjoyed listening to Casino Royale. The boat was more comfortable for sleeping and we both slept better that night.

10th January 2010

Beech Boys' Blog

The first few days into the crossing have taken all our time to settle into the routine of rowing shifts, new sleep patterns and life on-board an ocean rowing boat. Things have gone well on the whole. The sea was pretty lumpy at the start and eventually the strong northwest wind took us towards Africa which wasn't the plan! So we went onto the para-anchor to stop drifting that way and waited for the winds to turn more easterly. In the end we spent two nights and a day on para-anchor. We were tired and the rest was useful, such as it was. But two big people in the cabin when the boat is being rocked around in the waves is not fantastic. Joe the swimmer didn't feel well and was off his food - he said everything tasted of plastic!

We are currently making our way in light winds down to 22 degrees north which should take another few days. Hopefully we can head more easterly with the trade winds after that.

Ship's Log

The sunrise was absolutely beautiful. The winds were light, and from the north. We have been making progress south, going with the gentle winds and waves, and we are hoping to catch northeasterly winds soon. James is feeling much better. He spotted a very big tanker on the horizon, but it passed well clear. We produced and sent a blog to Ann Kite at the University of Birmingham Sport to go onto our webpage and also to Christine, who had an extensive email contact list of supporters who we said we would keep in touch with. This was our first blog from the ocean, and James was able to download all our email messages. Reading them out took a while, as we had a week's worth to catch up with. They were really fun and encouraging to receive. We opened Sandra Hoving's surprise box today and appreciated the effort she put into this. We decided to open one parcel each Sunday as a morale booster.

Each day as we open our food bag, we enjoy reading Christine's messages enclosed with our food rations. Today we got her joke of the day about a mushroom being a fun-guy to be with! In the middle of the afternoon we thought we heard a splash and looking around saw some movement in the water. After a few moments we were amazed to see a small whale surface next to us and then proceed to make an impressive noise as it exhaled, with a spray of water flying into the air! It didn't stay long, just giving us a quick stare before submerging once again. We were unable to get the camera in time to take a photo. The afternoon was predominantly cloudy, but every so often the sun made it through and suddenly it would feel hot - a taste of things to come. We continued with our south-southwesterly course.

11th January 2010

Beech Boys' Blog

The night sky was fantastic, with some spectacular shooting stars and at times when not windy, totally peaceful. There is only a crescent moon these days which rises very late, a few hours before dawn, so with a cloudy night last night it was very dark. Inky black waves made themselves known to us with a lifting of the boat, or a splash of water. There is a strong east-northeast wind today, about 20 knots of wind speed. So we made good progress in the right direction!

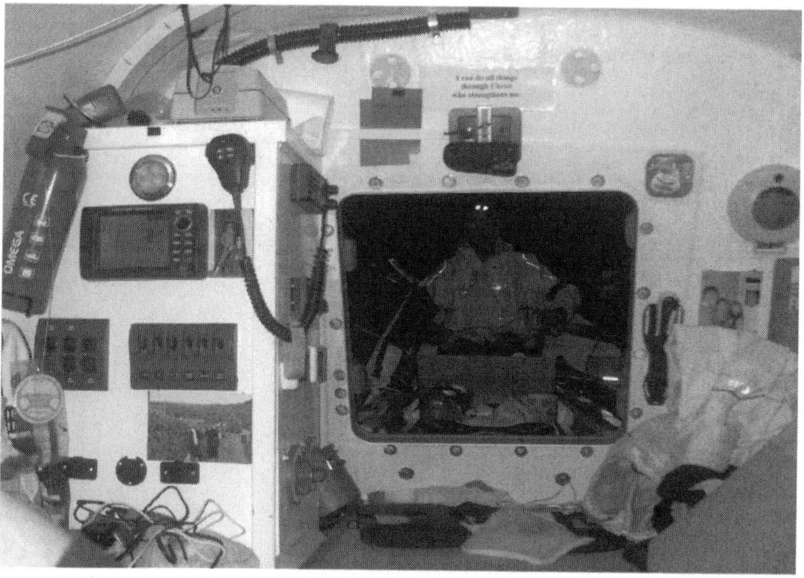

Night view out of cabin

Ship's Log

We now have 20 knots of easterly wind, which is blowing us in exactly the right direction for waypoint 3. We are pleased to have the tailwind, but as the sea builds there are some big waves to get used to. The definition of what a big wave is keeps changing as we encounter larger waves through the day! We estimate the waves are around 35 feet high.

'Beech Boys' is incredibly buoyant and we happily bob up and over waves rather like a cork. As the stern of 'Beech Boys' is lifted by the wave, from the rowing position you find yourself sat with your feet now higher than the rowing seat with the boat held for an instant on the slope of the wave face. The top of the wave then looms larger before fully emerging above the outline of the solar panels fixed on top of the cabin face. We feel safe on 'Beech Boys', despite the size of the waves. It is impressive to see how favourably our boat responds to the conditions.

In the evening we spoke to Christine on the satellite phone. I rowed a four hour shift first in the evening to help James get a break. We then rowed in two hour shifts through the night. The waves were challenging in the dark, but good progress was being made. Overnight we listened to 'Diamonds are Forever' on the iPod. The stars were fantastic again and the Milky Way absolutely spectacular.

12th January 2010

Ship's Log

The wind direction and strength remains the same and we continue to keep rowing directly downwind. James is eating biscuits and feeling better, which is good. It has been hot and sunny, with no cloud throughout the day. We decided to deploy the drogue so that we could both sleep for longer, but unfortunately got one of the karabiners caught between the rudder and the stern of the boat. I rowed the boat round into the wind and James, leaning out of the stern hatch, managed to free the karabiner, but we did get a small amount of water into the cabin, which was frustrating, since we were tired and we had to mop it up. We got some sleep overnight, but with the hatches closed, there was a lot of condensation in the cabin. At least we were getting blown in the right direction.

Following sea

13th January 2010

Beech Boys' Blog

After two days of strong east-northeast wind we are tired with the concentration of handling the changing wave sizes, which interestingly don't all come from the same direction! So no blog yesterday as there are too many other boat jobs to sort. Last night we rowed until midnight and then trailed a drogue behind the boat, so she stayed stern onto the waves and we sort of drifted in the right direction. This meant we both got a little more sleep, but the cabin only just works for two people to sleep at the same time. We were joking about the plan to put on extra weight before the row, as it now meant less space in the cabin!

We woke up to lighter winds of about 10 knots which made it more relaxing to row, but still plenty of waves to keep an eye on! The daily routine on 'Beech Boys' runs with a two hour watch of rowing or resting, or other jobs! These range from cleaning solar panels, checking battery levels, running the watermaker, sorting out meals and regularly tidying the cabin to keep some order to it!

Of course, we also have Joe the Swimmer to keep an eye on. He does well to keep up when we surf down a wave! So far the silicon supplement diet he has been on seems to be working and he hasn't complained of feeling poorly.

We played lots of "What does that cloud look like?" games. We have had crocodiles biting elephants' bottoms, Nemo blowing bubbles and lots of Simpsons clouds! You'll need to look at the credits to see what we mean next time The Simpsons are on TV.

<u>Ship's Log</u>

Once we recovered the drogue, the wind picked up and we had a good day of rowing. We both felt some benefit from having been on the drogue, but the cabin is so small with two of us in it, we probably won't do it again voluntarily! James is still finding it difficult with food and is going carefully with what he eats. We rowed through the night - there was no moon, but the stars looked great, and there were many shooting stars! Plankton can produce a phosphorescence when the water is disturbed - it is quite a bright light and on a couple of occasions we both thought we'd seen a ship's light, when in fact it was a phosphorescence flash, probably stirred up by fish. We had a few big waves break over the rear cabin and a few splashes in through the door, although thankfully nothing serious.

14th January 2010

<u>Beech Boys' Blog</u>

This is our tenth day at sea. Made some good progress overnight - top surfing speed so far 6.1 knots. Not as fast as your car we know, but your car isn't on the sea!

After lunch James spotted a sail on the horizon. We switched on our VHF radio and heard 'Aurora' transmitting a message for us as they were trying to locate us. After giving them our position, they finally met up for a chat about 3pm. They found it difficult to see us, due to the rough conditions, although with their 85 foot mast and sails we could see them a long way off! It was really good to see a yacht rather than a cargo ship. They sailed very close so we could chat to each other easily which was great. It was certainly a boost to have a friendly boat nearby.

We are waiting for today's visit by our friendly Storm Petrel, a sea bird that likes to fly around us in circles and see what we are up to. It would be interesting to know if it is the same one each time, but with no way of knowing we have accepted that it is! If we see much more of it we shall be on first name terms and perhaps able to offer it a job tidying up the cabin!

All equipment on-board continues to work well, which we are pleased about, as it would be a headache as well as time wasted having to make repairs. Battery levels all good, watermaker running well.

Ship's Log

The wind continues at 20 knots but is now more east-southeasterly, so all we can do today is travel west and try not to go northwest! The wind is forecast to drop over the next few days until Sunday, and we plan to get back into our night time rowing.

15th January 2010

Beech Boys' Blog

We have heard there is still snow at home in Coniston. We have our own interesting weather phenomena each breakfast time in the form of a micro snowstorm! Christine had carefully packed Ready brek into vacuum sealed sachets for us, to which we add powdered milk and sultanas and rehydrate it with boiling water. It is tricky trying to keep the Ready brek in the bowl when it is windy. Today as I looked up from my bowl I found Frosty the Snowman rowing the boat! James was covered with the Ready brek snow! We found some rehydrated carrot from last night's meal and with this as a nose the transformation was complete!

Last night's row was hard going. We found that it is actually possible to row while asleep for a few moments! It is a cloudy day today and not so windy. It has occurred to us that what we need is a good rowing song. So if you have nothing better to do over the weekend, how about putting some lyrics to Tony Christie's 'Is This the Way to Amarillo?' but change it to 'Is This the Way to Antigua?' It could be a good sing along song for the voyage!

Ship's Log

The lighter winds are now noticeable. We phoned Christine during the afternoon. At about six o'clock we saw some small dolphins close to the boat. Encouragingly, today is the first day James has managed to eat three meals.

16th January 2010

Beech Boys' Blog

We saw our first turtle and it followed along with us for a little while. We also had a fly on-board! We tried to check if it had a valid ticket for the accommodation, but they are hard to keep up with! We both had a hair wash and clean up this afternoon which was very refreshing. We also did some laundry.

As evening set in, after a fantastic ball of red sun descended below the horizon, the new moon appeared above the final red glow of the sunset. Although it was a crescent moon we could see the faint silver circle of the rest of it - incredibly beautiful. Overnight a lot of dew accumulates on the boat, and although we are attached onto the boat with a safety line, we have to be careful what we step on as what had been dry is now very wet. When we finish our rowing shift our clothes are damp, more from the dew than the perspiration!

Ship's Log

Today we swapped the food with a different day's food bag, as we really fancied some boil-in-the-bag meals, as opposed to the dehydrated ones we were having. James had Lancashire hotpot and I had vegetable curry. These tasted really good - more like normal food! James' appetite is certainly getting better.

We feel our rowing progress is getting slower and wonder if we might be in a countercurrent? After plotting our position on the chart we decided that as we were on the southerly edge of the 'corridor' we wanted to row along we would set up our next way point position 20 degrees north and 30 degrees west onto the GPS chartplotter. We are now rowing to that point, which is only 504 nautical miles away! Approximately 10 days rowing.

Overnight it was very cloudy. I found this particularly difficult as it meant I couldn't see the stars to steer by, and found it difficult to see GPS repeater in the night-time gloom.

17th January 2010

Beech Boys' Blog

While rowing along James saw in the distance the black shape of a whale breaching. It came virtually clean out of the water and landed with a huge splash. A long way off, but impressive enough. Progress over the water has slowed somewhat with quieter conditions now, but the miles are being ticked off!

We have been thinking that as people scour holiday brochures at this time of year for ideas we would produce a 'holiday magazine description' of our own accommodation:

Self-catering accommodation - provides excellent sea views, only a short step to the sea, dining room with unrivalled views of sunrise and sunset. Amenities - fitted self-cleaning kitchen, if you don't wipe the surfaces, a wave will do it for you! En suite bathroom - terrific view from the loo seat! Central heating controlled by window open, or closed. Full access to own private gym equipment, notably a bespoke rowing machine. Seafood easily obtained locally. Room service is available by prior arrangement with the other resident. Top tip from our guide writer - if you have run out of holiday ideas you are guaranteed to never forget this! Although with charming location, limited storage may be a problem for some, so only take essentials.

Ship's Log

Light east-southeasterly winds. The rowing still seems slow. During the early morning we used the cleaver blades which helped us push on a bit, but became difficult to use as soon as the sea turned choppy. After lunch we picked up 0.4 knots of extra speed, so maybe we are now back in a more helpful current? In the afternoon James sat on deck and read out the messages we had received on email. It was really good stuff, a real morale boost for us. We now have a moth on-board! Once again we don't know quite where our visitor has come from! Two dolphins surfaced near us this afternoon - always fun to watch.

18th January 2010

Beech Boys' Blog

Here we are two weeks into the row. Life on-board 'Beech Boys' is pretty much an established routine now. It is really important to maintain the framework and focus for each day and to keep on top of things. The toughest parts of the day are the two hour night shifts. Having rowed for two hours you are keen to sleep, but valuable sleeping time is eaten into as you get a drink and a snack and sort gear in the cabin, and then do the same before going back on watch again. However, being used to the noise of the boat as it passes through the water, the sound of waves hitting the boat and the movement the boat makes does help to get you to sleep quickly. Night-time rowing should start to become easier with more moonlight. The last few nights have been cloudy and no moon. You are surrounded with the night and the sound of waves, with only the glow of the navigation lights reminding you where you are. It wouldn't seem so bad if you only had to row one night shift, but having virtually twelve hours of night means we both have three shifts to do. However, the night has its own magnificence and you certainly have a sense of place being out here and seeing the vastness of the galaxy above.

We are continually aware that a huge amount of support for the row is underway and want to acknowledge these efforts with a 'hoot of praise!' Janet Vickers, from Sheffield Hallam University, brings sports degree students to the Raymond Priestley Centre where I work. Janet acknowledges special effort and achievement with an owl hooter! Not having such a thing with us, we are going to use our foghorn to give a hoot of appreciation from 'Beech Boys' for supporting efforts. So as we are two weeks in, there are a couple of hoots to be made! One goes to Ann Kite for keeping our web page and blog info up to date and for finding such good pictures.

Others go to three groups fundraising for WaterAid with us by rowing the same distance on their gym ergos - Lakes Leisure Ulverston, Greens Gym Sheffield with Vicky's rowing team and the group at the Munrow Sports Centre, University of Birmingham Sport. Brilliant! Thank you to all.

Ship's Log

The wind has dropped to become light and variable. The sea seems to be all over the place and it is difficult to get in a rhythm with our rowing. It is very frustrating seeing our progress slip back. During the day, four ships registered on our AIS; three cargo vessels and in the early evening a sailing boat 'Sunrise Ace'. We decided to go back onto a course to waypoint 3 and take advantage of what wind there is. After 9pm the wind strengthened and we needed good concentration particularly during our changeovers in the dark.

We now have a dragonfly as well as the moth on-board!

19th January 2010

Beech Boys' Blog

As it got dark the wind picked up and put us back on track overnight. Some larger waves burst and fizzed down the sides of 'Beech Boys' as we made progress in the dark. It is certainly easier taking advantage of free energy from the waves in the daylight when you can time your strokes to best advantage. So we are hopeful of getting more than 50 miles in during the next 24 hours.

After commenting on holidays in the weekend blog we were surprised to have our first visitors - a moth and a dragonfly. They obviously fancied something different and came on spec, taking bargain flights with FlyBee. They said they thought the place sounded as though there was a buzz to it and were keen to see for themselves. They left today and we hope nothing larger turns up. If we have an elephant wanting to see round, the ***tusk*** of rowing to Antigua will become considerably harder!

Ship's Log

The wind continues at 15 to 20 knots, pushing us southwest towards satellite phone four, which is more encouraging.

20th January 2010

Beech Boys' Blog

Oceanic All Stars 3 - Beech Boys 0. That was the result of this morning's first leg qualifier for the Atlantis Cup. Having played well throughout the duration of the overnight match, 'Beech Boys' conceded three late goals. The Oceanic All Stars brought on their substitute Wavio Sploshisuki from Japan with devastating results. In ten minutes he had scored a hat-trick, providing the Oceanic All Stars with a healthy lead ahead of the return fixture in Coniston. Wavio's first goal really went against the run of play, as he swept in over the port side and devastated a newly made bowl of porridge. While the 'Beech Boys' began to tidy up this hole in their defence, almost immediately Wavio appeared on the starboard side and with a delicately curled pass brought a wave around the stern cabin to expose the defensive frailty of the kitchen. The stove was extinguished, the pan was knocked over and in the chaos, the lid was lost overboard! Joe the swimmer wanted to go after it, but the lid was nowhere to be seen. The final goal, which will surely be favourite to win this month's wave of the month competition, was extraordinary. Wavio blasted in from the halfway line, an incredible wave that came straight over the rear cabin to take out the rest of the breakfast stuff and completely soaked the 'Beech Boys'.

So as you can see, a tricky start to the morning! However, at least the final wave cleared away most of the spilled porridge!

We now think we have an answer to the insect visitors to the boat. One of our sponsors, Bunches Internet Florist, has a floral logo. We have this on the main cabin and also on the oars, so they obviously feel at home when they see the flowers!

We have with us a supply of Jelly Babies and there is now some romantic news to report regarding Joe the swimmer and the Yellow Jelly Baby! To begin with we thought that Yellow Jelly was just feeling ill, as she was always looking over the side of the boat. It now turns out this was to get a better view of Joe! More news to follow as and when it becomes available.

Ship's Log

It is hard keeping up with the daily mileages that we were aiming for, although we are working very hard to do this. We phoned Christine this afternoon and she was worried we wouldn't have time for a holiday in Antigua, with the flights home already booked. The crescent moon is getting larger, giving more light to row by. It is interesting to see that as soon as the sun goes down, the moon appears over the horizon, a bit like celestial juggling!

21st January 2010

Beech Boys' Blog

What will I have for my evening meal tonight? The all important subject of food! Meals on 'Beech Boys' are mainly freeze dried, for instance chilli con carne or chicken tikka. The meal is in a foil packet to which you add water and there you have 900 calories! We also have as a contrast boil-in-the-bag meals. These weigh more since they are hydrated and have more texture, so are more enjoyable to eat. The dehydrated meals are just very soft to eat, but do have more calories. We have managed to keep up with eating our main meals. Our breakfast has been porridge with sultanas and honey and a muesli bar broken into it. We have enjoyed these breakfasts as they are pretty normal.

We also have a lot of snacks to give a boost between main meals. We are currently not keeping up with the planned snack intake! Partly because we did not manage to eat a lot during the first part of the row as it was rough and we started to develop a backlog of snacks. So far we haven't eaten as much chocolate as we thought we would! Things we have enjoyed have been beef jerky, as it is chewy and a little salty. We also have some specialised products from PowerBar. Energizer bars have gone down well, particularly during night -time rowing shifts. They are chewy and make you feel as though you have eaten more than you have. The PowerBar rehydration drinks powder is being used each day. It livens up the taste of the desalinated water and helps with muscle recovery. We are pleased that muscle soreness hasn't been a problem - although you do get a numb bum by the end of a two hour shift. We often perform various 'on-seat jiggles' to help circulation and keep comfortable. Lots of Sudocrem is also being strategically applied! Hands are holding up well, largely down to good gloves.

During these last couple of days we have been puzzled with slower boat speed. After four bottlenose dolphins had been with us for 30 minutes we decided to check out the hull. Barnacles! Lots of them! So I went over the side and did the underwater equivalent of scraping ice off a car windscreen to remove them. This was tiring work. There was a lot of growth to scrape off and as 'Beech Boys' was being lifted on the waves I was being dragged through the water. I was holding onto the grab line with one hand and using the other to apply the scraper. I had to swap hands every so often as one arm or the other became tired from the effort. The end result was a clean hull and we now have better boat speed as we travel around one knot faster for the same effort. It certainly explains why we felt we were slowing down over the past week. When we get a quiet moment we will check this again, but it will probably become a weekly job from now on.

Cleaning the hull

<u>Ship's Log</u>

James has had to dismantle and clean the gas burner as it had stopped working after the soaking it received from the waves yesterday. Fortunately he succeeded in getting it going again, so we will still be able to have hot meals! We had ravioli boil-in-the-bag for tea, which was wonderful. We both agreed we could have eaten this meal several times over!

22nd January 2010

Beech Boys' Blog

We found our first flying fish on deck this morning! It was a small one, only two inches long, so too small to eat! Apparently they can be expected for the rest of the crossing now. There are large Dorado fish next to the boat, and their silvery blue scales pick up the bright sunlight in a dramatic fashion. They jump out of the water from time to time - we would have a great meal if one landed in the boat!

Returning to food thoughts from yesterday, we do have a treats bag, which we have dipped into. Food is a great motivator. We have also appreciated finding surprises stowed in our daily food bag. Jill and Warren - your oatcakes were great! Grandma Morrow - we have loved your Christmas cake which Christine vacuum packed - it tastes really good at 3.30am!

As we move into the weekend we are looking forward to some Christmas food on our re-run of Christmas. We will open the food bags originally expected for use on Christmas Day. There are some small presents on-board which will be fun to open too! We will let you know Grandma Beech how the Christmas pudding and tinned cream go down!

We are really hoping for some easterly winds now. We have been navigating within a 100 mile wide 'corridor' to take best advantage of winds, but don't need to go much further south after the weekend. If the winds stay northeast we will have to row across them at an angle until we get the favoured easterly.

Well, off to the loft now to find some Christmas decorations! They should set things up for the Christmas Day at sea that we missed because of the late start.

Ship's Log

We both feel the night-time rowing is getting better, apart from getting up to start the shift. Although the previous night I had fallen asleep while rowing! The winds are still north-easterly and the forecast from Woodvale is that low pressure and north-northwesterly winds are due, which is bad news. We keep going southwest in the hope of avoiding this weather and being stuck on para-anchor. After our earlier experience we are keen to avoid time on para-anchor if we can. We are keeping careful track of our position each day to help us decide on the best route. We washed our clothes today, and phoned my mum, then Johan for weather information.

23rd to 25th January 2010

Beech Boys' Blog

It's windy, over 20 knots of wind and our new surfing record is now 7.9 knots. The weekend weather has redefined our big wave scale. All waves previously described as big have now been downgraded to 'biggish', as the ocean has now introduced us to some 'big waves'. One thing is for sure. There will always be another wave out there, rolling along, waiting to surprise, to loom large with a foaming crest and steal the coveted title of 'big wave'.

Food bag number 19 would have contained our Christmas Day rations if we had started on the original date of 6th December. However with seawater streaming over the deck and across the deck hatches it was difficult getting this Christmas food bag out. In the end we didn't find everything, so some more treats to come when we can check properly. We ended up finding Day 8's food bag, which somehow must have been hidden, and we had sausages and beans followed by a tin of peaches for lunch. The Christmas puddings from Grandma Beech were brilliant! Thank you.

Houses moving along with you as you walk down the street! It has become a constant image as we view the waves rolling up behind us. The 'watery houses' have been going in our direction which has helped progress, but we decided to use a drogue on Saturday night as we didn't fancy rowing in the dark with some of these waves around in case we accidentally ended up broadside onto one, with the associated risk of capsize. The drogue looks like a triangular reinforced shopping bag, open at two ends. It is dragged behind the boat and its resistance through the water is sufficient to keep the stern into the waves and stops the boat accidentally surfing down one out of control.

After setting 'Beech Boys' onto the drogue we both crammed into the cabin to get some sleep. After only a few minutes I was struggling. It was really unpleasant to be in the stuffy atmosphere. I found it difficult to breathe and made the decision to escape. I couldn't go far, but I knew I needed to be out of the cabin. I would sleep outside on deck. I clipped myself on and sat on the rowing seat nearest the cabin to get some shelter and I held onto the oars, which were tied onto the oar rests, in order to give me some stability. Thankfully James was able to settle in the cabin.

It was noisy on deck and 'Beech Boys' rolling about made the task of drifting into sleep rather elusive. When sleep came it was fitful, but I was worried that this might become a regular problem to deal with. I remembered a Bible verse shared with us before we set off. 'Do not be discouraged. I am with you wherever you go'. Sleep eventually took its hold and after one longer spell of sleep I felt significantly better and was able to return to the cabin with no problems. I slept for the rest of the night.

Mileage has been good with the following sea, but we have had updated forecast of winds turning against us, so will have to see how this develops.

We are now into week three and hope to benefit from the east to west ocean current towards the end of the week. This should provide some added boat speed which will be appreciated! We are both taking things very much one day at a time and trying to keep a focus on the needs of the day. With still a long way to go, keeping a clear goal for each day is important. Trying to row southwest seems very slow going at the moment.

We have had some laughs remembering top funny TV moments. Last night, James remembered Todd Carty skating out of the rink during 'Dancing on Ice' which we chuckled over for a while! That's it for today - sorry to have three days in one, but weather makes it hard to stay in the cabin to write for too long.

24th January 2010

Ship's Log

At 7am we came off the drogue. James helped by rowing towards it, as I pulled in the line. James saw a flying fish today. It is amazing how far they can travel, and at considerable speed!

We have had a few "What film does this remind you of?" moments. While getting breakfast ready, we talked about the view we had been able to see out of the stern hatch. The metal edge of the hatch is a perfect picture frame for the moon in the night sky. James asked "What film did that remind you of?" It had to be 'Apollo 13', as the astronauts view the moon from their capsule window and gaze on in wonder at what it would be like to walk on the surface.

As we sat on deck preparing lunch, we had an exciting moment as a big wave under the 'new' category swept around the stern and straight across the deck. As it foamed around the cabin, it filled the central cockpit like a bath! So for a moment only the two cabins were above the surface. In that instant we were both sat in the ocean, surrounded by water until 'Beech Boys' lifted and the water drained out of the scuppers. We quickly grabbed pans, bowls and cups to prevent them being washed away. “What film does this remind you of?!” asked James. It had to be ‘Mary Poppins’ when the gun is fired on the roof of the house and everyone holds onto pictures and vases to stop them breaking! Anyway, nothing lost which was surprising, considering what had just happened! We just had to start over again preparing lunch!

25th January 2010

Ship’s Log

It was good to talk to Christine on the phone this evening and find out that we had covered 46 miles in the previous 24 hours! The winds calmed down in the late evening and overnight. We opened Sandra’s crackers, party poppers and balloons. James put the balloons on our spare oars overnight. There was good moonlight, but as a result fewer stars were visible. Once the moon drops below the horizon the stars are brilliantly bright until the dawn light once again extinguishes them. We continue to boil water each day and put it into flasks for that day’s meals. Reading our emails made us laugh as the headline in the North West Evening Mail referred to us having experienced a snowstorm - a misunderstanding from our blogs - in fact we had been talking about porridge and milk powder which had been blown around in the strong wind!

The Bible verse - Isaiah 41:10 ‘Fear not for I am with you, be not dismayed for I am your God, I will help you, I will strengthen you, I will uphold you with my victorious right hand' has been a real encouragement and has helped maintain motivation. I have really enjoyed listening to 'Delirious?' and 'YFriday' on James' iPod during the night-time rowing. We are staying positive and motivated, anticipating that we have another 40 days at sea to meet our predicted crossing time of around 60 days.

26th January 2010

Beech Boys' Blog

We have really appreciated the level of support from everyone. All the messages are fantastic to receive and are very motivating - a MASSIVE thank you.

Joe and Yellow Jelly Baby are still getting on well although talk of marriage may be too early to report at this stage. Yellow Jelly did audition originally for the Spice Girls, but was not 'tangy' enough. Later she was told she was too sweet for the SugarBabes! Anyway, her career seems to be taking off now in 'EastEnders'. She has a small part playing a Jelly Baby - apparently she waves from the top of the paper bag after someone has gone into the newsagents to buy a quarter of Jelly Babies. Look out carefully to see if you can spot her!

Hoots of praise from the 'Beech Boys' foghorn for Sandra Hoving - really good to have your box of surprises to open every so often. We loved the neon light balloons! Thanks also to Coniston Crusaders for all your messages. HOOT! HOOT!

Ship's Log

Today we found the Christmas chocolates that Christine has packed for us! Hurray! However, the wind and waves are now across our path, making progress southwest to waypoint 4 very slow. It is now tedious at times as we can't get 'Beech Boys' to run. The waves hit the oars and upset our rowing strokes. Winds are not against us but are pushing us north and we want to travel west. This morning with the swell and wind direction across us we did half a mile in one hour! Looking better now, but if we do 15 miles today it will be a good effort.

Bad weather is forecast to hit from the northwest for Thursday through to Saturday. So we are trying to push west and hope to avoid getting blown north today and tomorrow. It looks like a couple of days ahead on para-anchor and a loss of momentum to our voyage! James and I cleaned the barnacles off the hull of the boat doing one half each. After swimming in the sea and washing, we both felt refreshed. We also washed our clothes, so pleasant aromas were wafting from 'Beech Boys'! An email from WaterAid told us that Radio Cumbria would like to interview us via satellite Phone on Friday for their Breakfast Show. So we will need to have our phone on early on Friday. Radio Cumbria has followed us through our preparations, so it will be good to keep this going.

27th January 2010

<u>Beech Boys' Blog</u>

After rowing through to 4am this morning we decided to go onto the para-anchor. We had been crawling along barely making headway. On each rowing stroke the boat speed didn't register on the satnav display. The feedback it gave us was a constant 0.0 knots and we decided the effort was greater than the gain. The forecast for these south-southwest winds has been correct, but it looks as though we could experience these for the next five days! Anyway at least we had a longer sleep last night. I hoped I would not have the recurrence of the breathing problems from a few days ago.

We still have to decide the best course of action for the rest of this week. We think we will row together just to make some progress each day and then sleep through the night deploying the para-anchor to reduce drift, rather than row in shifts. Rowing together gives some extra power which will hopefully be greater than the wind and waves opposing us. Certainly if the wind gets stronger then we will have to accept that we stay on the para-anchor all the time. Frustrating stuff! It is actually a pleasant sunny day and if the wind was blowing from the east we would be skipping along but it isn't!

The hatch into the main cabin from the deck is about 1.5 feet square, so getting in and out of the cabin requires some care. The main techniques used so far are to enter head first crawling style with a half-turn once your waist is through so you can then sit on the cabin mattress, remove your shoes and then pull your feet in. Alternatively, face away from the door, sit into the space and shuffle your bottom far enough in that you can then duck your head through the hatch. When done wearing waterproofs and an uninflated life jacket it is a serious test of one's flexibility! Leaving the cabin is usually done feet first so you can put your shoes on with your feet out of the cabin. Then by holding the grab handle above the hatch a limbo style is adopted to bring the rest of your body out of the cabin! As with all gymnastic movements there is a grace and ease to it when it goes well, but looks very funny if it goes wrong.

Some basic Do's and Don'ts. If losing balance, still point your toes. If you hit your head or shin, keep smiling and make it look like it is part of your routine. Make sure you have unclipped your safety line before entering cabin to prevent embarrassing reversing actions to unclip. There is certainly scope for some sort of sport to be developed from this, possibly using a gymnast's ribbon or ball! To throw a ball out of the hatch, exit and then catch the ball without falling overboard would be total mastery of the art!

Thanks Alan and Glenda for the surprises in our food bags! Also thanks to Johan for helping us with weather updates which have been really helpful.

We will do our best to get the green dot moving on the computer screen over these next days.

Ship's Log

Although it is a sunny day the wind is strengthening and waves are increasing in size. We went on deck for our evening meal at sunset. Tough night in the cabin, it was rough and we were rolled around a lot and woken by waves hitting the boat. The cabin was very stuffy and we ran the gauntlet of opening the hatches to get air through while avoiding splashes from the waves. The tea towel comes in handy to mop up when the sea gets in!

28th January 2010

Beech Boys' Blog

As the winds are still south-southwest all boats in the race are stuck on para-anchor. So (excuse the pun) we are all in the same boat!

Extract from Woodvale Challenge race website: 'Crews have now been at sea for three weeks and spirits are generally high across the fleet. While all competitors have had to overcome problems, be they physical, electrical or mechanical, all are managing to continue on towards Antigua. It has been said on more than one occasion that rowing across an ocean is not simply a physical endeavour. It summons all available skills and thoughts to overcome problems that could manifest themselves. For many, the physical problems can override everything and to cope it is essential to find a cure that works best for the individual, whether that be adjusting weight distribution and balance on the seat to minimise discomfort or changing how one lies in the cabin to move with the boat as she lists and rolls in the ocean.

Perhaps one of the most gruelling decisions of the fleet was that of Limited Intelligence. After losing a crew member so early in the race it would be easy to stop, turn round and go straight back to the Canaries. However, they took the brave decision to carry on to Antigua and are now nearly 700nm into this incredible challenge.

To date, between the 30 crews that started the race and Britannia III the record attempt, over 23000nm have been made good, almost 750 per crew. Several crews are inside pace for a record or race record, and no doubt all crews and supporters are logging and recording mileage, not just to compare against other crews in the fleet, but to ascertain a completion date.

What is arguably the most incredible feat of the race so far is that all the crews that started the race are still on the ocean, rowing to Antigua. The race is now at a stage where there is no turning back - the only way to finish is to finish. While the two support yachts will closely follow the fleet and attend any situation, they will only go as fast as the slowest crew. That is to say no matter what happens to the sores, or the aching muscles, the quickest way to Antigua is to row, no matter how long it takes. All the time a crew can row they will get closer and closer to the finish. While the weather will change, and morale will fluctuate crews should try to keep the belief and remember the overriding goal - to row across an ocean'

Ship's Log

On para-anchor, the cabin is stuffy, we haven't eaten lots. No blog entry because I didn't feel able to write this in the cabin. If the waves are quieter for a few minutes we have been on deck for fresh air. Although we are both feeling it could be worse! Proverbs 3:5-6 'Trust in the Lord with all your heart'...and 'Delirious' song 'Every little thing (is going to be all right)' both provide encouragement. Weather forecast shows westerly winds for another five days. We are praying for easterly winds to move us out of here. We listened to a Bond book on James' iPod speakers tonight. I have developed tendonitis in the middle finger of my left hand. I hope this enforced rest from rowing will aid a quick recovery.

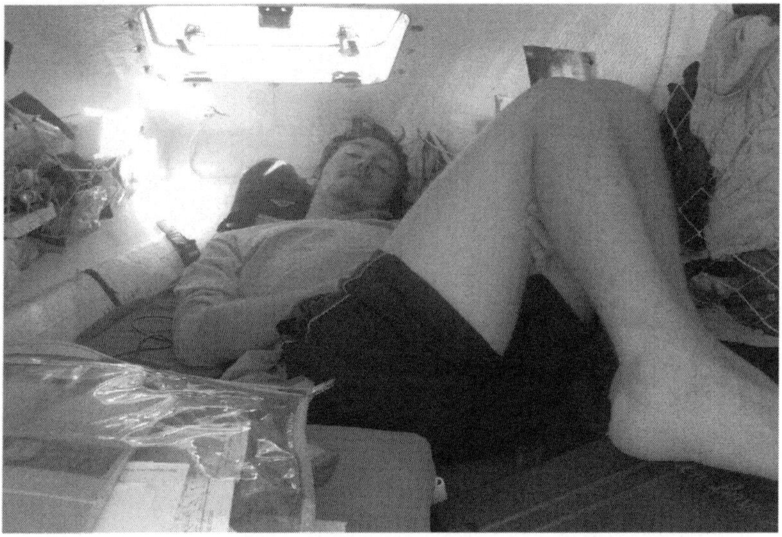

Resting in the cabin

29th January 2010

Ship's Log

We had the satellite phone on but didn't receive the call from Radio Cumbria. We spoke to Christine on Satellite phone in evening. It was good to hear from Christine that we are drifting in a positive direction, despite wind being against us! The para-anchor must be in a current moving us the right way! This is our 25th day at sea.

30th January 2010

Beech Boys' Blog

This evening we asked Christine to write a message to go onto our blog, reassuring readers that despite being on the para-anchor, we are in good spirits and reserving our energy to start rowing again when the winds are in a better position, which hopefully will be on Monday.

We were sitting out on deck facing each other this evening eating our meal. While James was appreciating the beauty of the sunset that was behind me on the western horizon I was looking in the opposite direction and admiring the full moon coming up over the horizon! Wonderful.

We have both grown beards over the last few weeks! Christine told James to take photos since she has never seen either of us with a beard before!

<u>Ship's Log</u>

Ship Ahoy!

We had an AIS alert warning us of a ship nearby. I was on deck and spotted a container ship. It was coming our way. The vessel belongs to Grimaldi Lines. We had seen one of her sister ships when we took 'Beech Boys' to Tilbury Dock. James called them up on VHF as they were passing close. In the end they were only 700 metres away from us and we could see men out on deck. The smell of the diesel fumes reached across to us! After they had passed they called us back on the radio and asked "Beech Boys, are you alright?" James explained we were on para-anchor waiting for the wind to change so we could carry on rowing to Antigua. "OK", came the reply - we heard nothing else from them! This evening we had chicken and dumplings, a boil-in-the-bag meal, followed by tinned pineapple. Delicious! We listened to another Bond book on the iPod for a bedtime story.

31st January 2010

Beech Boys' Blog

Yes! We are still here on the para-anchor! The wind continues to blow strongly from the west, so we are captive here in mid -ocean until the easterlies return, possibly late on Monday or Tuesday morning. At least the para-anchor has found a friendly current which despite the winds has given us some positive mileage south! Hurray!

We don't like being on para-anchor too much. The boat moves very differently from when it is underway normally. Waves can hit the front hatch so that needs to be shut to keep the water out and although we do have two cabin ventilators it still gets very hot and stuffy. Even though it has meant catching some waves I have preferred to be on deck much of the day, while James finds the odd motion of the boat upsets his stomach and has tended to lie still in the cabin. Night-time is not so bad. We have adopted a 'heads and feet at opposite ends' approach and this seems to work, but with two tall people in such a small cabin, changing position has to be co-ordinated in order to avoid getting a toe in your ear! Every so often we carefully open the hatch to get a cooling draft through the cabin and this helps reduce condensation. However, we have kept up the daily routine of operating the watermaker, making three meals and keeping the batteries charged. This was quite hard the first day we were on para-anchor, as we were adjusting to the new situation we were likely to be in for the next week and mentally coming to terms with the enforced stop.

We have definitely lost weight! Our efforts to put weight on before the row were important. We are probably around our normal weight now, so going subnormal weight from now on! Although eating well, we are aware that more recently we have not finished all the food allocated as snacks for that day.

Ship's Log

We opened one of Sandra's presents today - tummy tablets for emergency relief. The waves turned big at teatime and I got soaked as I returned to the cabin. The door was on the latch so very little water went inside, it was just inconvenient to have wet clothes. The blog was restarted today.

1st February 2010

Beech Boys' Blog

We had a fun time reading through all the messages sent to us yesterday evening. They do reach us and we gain new motivation from receiving them - thank you.

The wind slowly turned to the north this morning as predicted, and this means that we should be able to get back on the oars in the next 24 hours. So today we are getting ourselves sorted to move on. We hope we might get away late afternoon or first thing Tuesday. James cleaned the hull of barnacles in readiness for us leaving para-anchor. It will be a great feeling to be off again. It was quite rough last night with some waves crashing heavily on the cabin. Despite the wind we are still drifting in the right direction! All systems are still working well on-board and the main cabin is now tidy and repacked. Now it's just a question of rowing 50 miles a day! This will be our target and with some fair wind and a favourable current we may do a bit better.

Thanks again to Mike, Jason and Don for your work on the boat. It is all coping well with the Atlantic conditions. Stove is all good too, Mike. You never know, you may have some people after your design, the race organisers were very impressed with it!

We were interested to hear that Bob Ketts from Furness Plastics, the company who produced all the sponsors' logos for the boat, is cruising on the 'Oriana' to the Caribbean. Bob, we will wait with interest to see if your course comes close to us. We think you may take a rhumb line from Madeira in which case you are likely to be north of us. Anyway a message from 'Oriana' would be brilliant! All the logos are still attached to the boat!

2nd February 2010

Beech Boys' Blog

After seven days on para-anchor we re-discovered the oars this morning. We came off para-anchor at 8.30am. The northwesterly wind is gentle and we have made progress across it to the southwest. We set a new waypoint: 19 degrees north, 40 degrees west, only 627 miles away! Our journey is on again. Do we still know how to row? What course was it again?! How does the steering work? We soon found answers to all these questions and it felt good to be underway! If we had known how long we were going to be on para-anchor we would have struggled to believe that we could cope with being in such a small space for that length of time. Each weather forecast suggested things would change in two days. Knowing we had previously spent two days in the cabin earlier in the voyage enabled us to believe we could do it again.

Ideally we need an east wind to push us westward. Currently, as we don't want to go south, we are rowing across the northerly wind and waves to progress to the west. It tends to be awkward as the boat is side on to the waves and the oars are seldom in the water at the same time. However, we are making progress and Antigua will be a few miles nearer by the end of the day. It will be interesting to see how quickly we adapt back to the two hour shift pattern and waking up in the night to row.

The end of the para-anchor stop concluded with something of a shock. Having washed clothes and threaded them along the oars to dry during the afternoon we were surprised to have a sudden rain shower. As the clothes were virtually dry I collected these in. One minute there were two pairs of Gill quick dry boxer shorts hanging up. I put one pair in the cabin then turned back for the other pair, but they were gone! A rapid check of the water around the boat showed no sign of them. Someone or something had stolen them!

We got in touch with the LOPD - Local Ocean Police Department - and they sent round a Sergeant Kipper and PC Cod to investigate. They arrived very swiftly and were helpful, although we did think Sergeant Kipper smoked too much. They think the disappearance could be linked to a series of thefts believed to be masterminded by gangster Mud C. Malone. If they could ***plaice*** him at the scene of the crime they would have him. The LOPD think his gang watch boats on para-anchor and then steal goods to order. In this case the quality Gill quick dry boxers would have been taken from the scene by flying fish courier and most likely are now on sale in a Paris or a Milan boutique! It is organised crime on a grand ***scale***. The Officers took some ***brief*** notes and said they would let us know if anything turned up. We commented that this sort of thing was going to put people off visiting their area, or indeed attempting an Atlantic row if their kit is being stolen. It is not what you expect. PC Cod showed us some lockable clothes pegs we could buy mail order which might stop the same thing happening again. Some kind tuna fish said they would set up a Neighbourhood Watch Scheme. Anyway it's one of those things we will have to put ***behind*** us and focus on the row ahead.

James read out our email messages today which were encouraging as always. We saw a large tanker called 'United Trader' pass on a parallel course, but travelling in the opposite direction, about two miles away. We saw a number of good sized flying fish today and opened more of Sandra's presents since the box had become soggy while on para-anchor due to water splashing into the cabin. We enjoyed eating the liquorice sticks and found that we have another pack of cards! We are both in good spirits. I feel there has been answered prayer regarding me being in the cabin, the Lord has certainly got me through all the days on para-anchor. God will make a way! We are getting back into the night-time rowing routine, at least the moonlight is good at the moment.

I have recently been getting a sharp pain in my side near my right armpit, so James prayed for me today. My left little finger has also been sore and has a tendency to lock up.

We decided to ration the camping gas and have only one hot meal a day. We were concerned that we may otherwise run out in 20 days, and we need to make it last at least another 40!

3rd February 2010

Beech Boys' Blog

Each morning we look forward to locating the food bag for that specific day. The bags are numbered from Day 1 to 90 and are distributed between eight watertight storage areas in the hull. Access to the storage area is via a circular screw-down hatch. The food bags were positioned in the boat so that we would take something from different storage areas on different days. This prevents the trim of the boat from being affected. Obviously if you eat all the food on one side of the boat first it would not be in balance until you had eaten everything from the other side! So this round robin approach kept the boat balance correct. So that we can locate specific bags, we have a food location plan which was drawn up by Christine and Pat when they packed and loaded all the supplies for us in La Gomera. They also put messages in each food bag for us. This gives us a daily supply of funny comments, a favourite Bible verse, or a reminder that we can do it! Keep going! It's good fun opening the bag to see what the meals and snacks will be for that day, as well as the message.

Today the excitement was high as we opened the snacks and discovered Grandma Morrow's Christmas cake and some chunks of marzipan! Marzipan is fantastic - the culinary equivalent of Play-Doh! I hasten to add that we do not normally play with our food, however creativity creeps in and the opportunity to make a row-through restaurant serving hot dogs is a must! In fact with a bit of imagination you can taste the sausage and onion and yes a bit of tomato sauce coming through now! Oh! Lost it - back to tasting of marzipan! But marzipan is still gooood! The food item James is most looking forward to in Antigua is hot buttered toast with Marmite! I am going more for the steak and potatoes and fresh vegetables! Anyway that is still some way off, but it is fun talking about favourite meals and places we have enjoyed eating out at over the years. Before long we will be remembering that classic rehydrated chicken tikka eaten mid -ocean!

Conditions on the ocean today are going well for us. Overnight we were still rowing across the waves, which wasn't too bad as the moonlight made it easy to spot any potentially bigger waves.

This morning the wind is more from the east so we have a slight following sea which is helping improve boat speed and makes rowing your shift more encouraging as you see the miles to go on the GPS display panel count down a little quicker. Only 1,800 nautical miles still to go.

Thank you to the Birch family for the effort put in to coming up with words for the verses to 'Is this way to Antigua'? Terrific!

Also good to hear that Christine is now officially a WAM! Wife And Mother of Ocean Rowers. Thanks for thinking that one up, Janet and Vicky!

4th February 2010

Beech Boys' Blog

Overnight the winds turned more northerly so we were again rowing across a brisk crosswind which slowed progress. As dawn broke the wind moved back to the east to give a more favourable tailwind. Although not strong, it moves us west which is good. I had an early morning shower as a heavy pulse of rain moved through. It finished just before James started his shift, so at least only one of us got wet! Rain is certainly a good antidote to falling asleep at the oars! Today is proving to be pretty overcast with the occasional shower thrown in, but certainly not cold.

We have now passed 20 degrees north 30 degrees west and are moving onto our next waypoint which is 550 nautical miles away. We are aiming to row 50 miles a day, so our next milestone should be reached in about 10 days with good conditions. We try and focus on making sure we get the best mileage we can from the conditions on the day, knowing these will fluctuate but hopefully even out in the end. It would be easy to be overwhelmed by the miles still to be covered without this 'one bit at a time' approach. We also enjoy the challenge of a daily target, along with the need to make sure you have done 'your bit' when it is your turn on the oars!

Although we have seen flying fish during the voyage, last night we had the first low flying, flying fish! As I was rowing a fish passed across the boat just in front of me, missing the spare oars on the oar supports by a few inches. We have now been visited by a representative of the Flying Fish Air Space Trust, or FFAST for short - no, we didn't know such an organisation existed either! Apparently all moving objects need to be correctly illuminated at night-time to show flying fish the safest crossing point. We asked if they meant 'a Pelican Crossing' but this didn't go down well as Pelicans eat fish! Nonetheless something like this is needed. We thought it best not to mention pressing buttons and traffic lights! In order to comply we will now have a couple of the neon light balloons we had leftover from Christmas tied on to the oars to provide the required safe crossing point. Crossing the ocean does not get easier with these peculiar regulations to comply with!

We had an interview today via satellite phone with Tyne Tees and Border News, which will be broadcast tonight. If you watch the Lookaround programme on Border ITV you will hear an update provided mid-ocean by James!

Ship's Log

It was good talking to Christine on the phone this evening. She told us that James' interview came across well and she was pleased she got a mention as James gave her a mid-ocean, "Hello Mum!"

5th February 2010

Beech Boys' Blog

Yesterday afternoon ended up being hot and sunny and the easterly wind stayed with us for most of the night which was great. Sunset was about 8.00pm and the first part of the night-time row was moonless, so it was good for looking at the stars. One of our changeover times is 1.30am. As James finished his shift and we got ready to change it was superb to see the first part of the moon rise over the horizon. The half-moon as it became visible was truncated horizontally and continued to rise into the sky in this gracefully relaxed position. At one point the moon went behind a cloud and produced a spectacular backlighting effect of silver light. As the moon reappeared, the iPod tune selection progressed from the pace of Chuck Berry's 'Johnny B. Goode' to Louis Armstrong's 'Wonderful World' - it was the perfect song for the moment as the moonlight found its way across the waves to touch the stern of the boat. Absolutely fantastic, even though my backside continuously reminds me it is in pain having been perched on a rowing seat for the last 32 days. We are getting better at pressing the mental 'pain delete' button to erase the reminder system our bodies are so good at generating. Thank goodness for Sudocrem!

Today we rowed in sunny and hot conditions. The wind was light and from a favourable direction, generating some small, but helpful waves which served to nudge us forward. We are now getting used to the ocean equivalent of motorbike outriders! We can clearly see in the water a couple of large brown fish that 'surf' inside the waves next to us and run along a parallel track. Occasionally if a larger wave has lifted the stern we can see them in the wave directly behind us. They obviously think we are going somewhere important and have decided to clear the way!

A question had cropped up from a previous blog regarding Joe the Swimmer and whether he was growing a beard too. Joe remains clean-shaven for purposes of streamlining for his swim. We do have to check him before he gets back in to swim to make sure he hasn't cut himself! Blood in the water is not advisable; even if the last time we spotted a shark was some 20 days ago.

We were really encouraged and amazed to read an email from Ann at University of Birmingham Sport, who enters our blog on to the web pages each day. Apparently over 2,500 people are now reading our blog! Part of the project is to let people know about the work of WaterAid and the idea with the blog was to help create interest. We are so pleased to learn it is so popular.

6th and 7th February 2010

Beech Boys' Blog

Friday afternoon ended up being our hottest day on the ocean so far, probably 45 degrees! The sky was completely cloudless and the wind had disappeared. The 'air conditioning' was therefore switched off as we had no breeze and this was pretty much the story overnight too. As the ocean became very calm James decided to have a swim to cool off and employed the barnacle scraper. As the boat was only moving on a gentle swell it was easier to work along the keel band this time. When the boat rises and falls it is easy to end up with a few bumps if you are underneath, so this was time well spent. James saw lots of Dorado fish in the water while his cleaning operations were underway. A large one, maybe four feet long jumped out of the sea, making big splashes next to us which was fun to watch. Just before sunset we spotted a whale some 100 metres behind us, but it was only with us a short while and never got closer. It was awesomely quiet with no noise from wind or wave as we watched the sunset. The last two days we wished we had following winds, as we had only managed 40 nautical miles, and we were really keen to get 50 plus miles each day.

Saturday 6th - late morning a gentle breeze helped to keep temperatures cooler and gave us a little push west. Some big fish were jumping again. They looked amazing in the air as they were so silvery blue, however their landings were never graceful - the John Smith top bombing advert springs to mind -

lots of splash and noise and that's about it. No elegance in the landing phase at all! We hope one of these doesn't land onboard - they would create some chaos as they must be pretty heavy! You assume they know where they are jumping!

Ship's Log

It is hot! Little breeze, gentle swell. We now seem to be in a westerly current, giving us between 0.5 and 1 knot. We are pleased about that - maybe we can break the 50 nautical mile barrier! We saw turtles today, quite small, about a foot in diameter. It was really good to speak to my sister Gill and her husband Mike this evening in New Zealand. We really enjoy the satellite phone and the way it connects us back to everyday life events. Dolphins were around us at 7pm and stayed for a while, James got a good photo! I used a couple of rubber pads on my left oar hand to create a larger handle diameter, which should help to reduce the problem with the tendons in my finger.

Good to have some breeze back today, particularly as we had fallen off the helpful current we picked up yesterday. It also made the hottest part of the day more manageable, with the cool of the breeze.

Over the weekend we had been thinking about the straight-forward nature of the row. How easy it is to be in the right place at the right time - you are either rowing or resting. You are either in the cabin or on the deck! It has to be said that resting does include everything on the boat apart from rowing - so sleeping, eating, washing clothes, chart/navigation work, blogging and communications, tidying and checking kit etc are all resting activities. However despite the easy division of these tasks we have been getting in a real muddle on when it is our turn to row again during the night! A number of times now one of us has come off the oars and gone to sleep in the cabin, only to re-emerge shortly after to check if it was our go again, as we thought we had slept through the alarm! Alternatively even coming out kitted up to row again, as we were sure the alarm had gone off! Why we have never checked the clock on these occasions we haven't been able to fathom. Anyway, it is better appearing too early for the next rowing shift than oversleeping!

A culinary treat - we discovered a tin of pineapple we had forgotten about. Wow! It tasted wonderful. Glad we remembered a tin opener! We also appreciated an Angel Delight whip. This was consumed more as a milk shake than a dessert, but it was really refreshing! As the advert used to say, "Happiness is a tin of fruit and an Angel Delight!" Well, words to that effect!

Light northerly winds overnight have settled to northeasterly now it is day time. We have lost our favourable current, but the wind is helping us. We didn't go over 50 nautical miles, but had the 8th highest mileage in the fleet, so not bad! Generally it has been a quiet day. We had an AIS contact with the ship 'African Halcyon'. We finally spotted her some miles away and were just able to see the top of the superstructure on the horizon. Overnight the fish underneath the boat were easy to see with our head torch.

8th February 2010

Beech Boys' Blog

It is fascinating how the ocean's rhythm of wave patterns and swell alters. Having become so calm with the absence of a breeze for a day, the overnight wind created a new set of wavelets on the ocean which are moving in the westward direction we are travelling. However, from the north there is a long swell, with waves about 200 metres apart. So we are rowing in two wave patterns, although all the swell is doing is gently lifting and lowering us. When we are at the bottom of the swell it is like being in a 200 metre wide saucer. The sides of the saucer being water and whichever way you look you are looking uphill, or 'up water'! When on the top of the swell our horizon is expanded and you really feel on top of everything - for a full three seconds at least! You can also see the other ocean saucers, or water craters around you. All very mesmerising!

The sliding seat we sit on when we row slides along a rail with skateboard wheels acting as the rollers. After 34 days at sea the bearings are becoming very noisy. Rather than have the wheels cease and the seat not roll, we have decided to go into the pits for a full bearing change. There are eight wheels and each wheel has two cassettes of bearings to change. We started the stopwatch to see how fast the change was. Thirty five minutes later we were off! You can see why in Formula 1 they have pit crews waiting with everything to hand, but maybe Formula 1 are missing a trick?! It could add extra drama and entertainment if the driver had to do his own mechanics. Even if he had to fill up with petrol at a normal garage type pump and run into the kiosk to pay! There could be some fun here with drivers forgetting which pump number they are paying the bill for. Even tactical paying - you could hold someone else up in the queue if you were refuelling at the same time by buying some sweets as well as paying for your petrol! What do you think, Mr Ecclestone?

Anyway we were glad we had all the new bearing cassettes already packed with grease before we left La Gomera and the right tools all to hand. No washers or nuts were lost through the scuppers and now we have a smooth running seat. If we have to do another change we now have a pit time to beat!

Ship's Log

Heavy overnight rain. James bore the brunt of this. Every time he was on the oars the rain got heavier - not particularly nice. There was no moon until very late into the night, so it was cloudy, very wet and dark. The foot strap on our foot-steering system came loose and needed to be retied, which we did during the changeover at first light.

The rationing of the Calor Gas continues. We now have one hot meal a day. We have three large gas containers left which we think should be enough. The winds are helping us make good progress during the night despite the rain.

9th February 2010

Beech Boys' Blog

The wind was steady from the northeast-east through yesterday and overnight, so we were able to take advantage of the waves going our way. It was fairly cloudy through the night, with rain at times, so with no moon until the very early morning it was a dark night. This morning we have favourable winds again, with a slightly unpredictable wave pattern meaning that every so often we have a side wave to contend with, or we have a larger steeper wave which hits the stern of the boat and sends spray flying towards the oarsman!

It seems that all the work we put into helping the flying fish has not made much difference. Despite the clear markings we now have for the fly-over, a few fish have tried a fly through! One even collided with the boat's VHF aerial and flew into the side deck. We assume they are OK. They certainly did not stop to see if they had done any damage. Maybe anxious not to lose their 'no **clams** bonus'?

A few young people from Coniston Crusaders have been asking about barnacles. They are part of the plankton that live in the sea - tiny organisms. As we move fairly slowly they are able to attach themselves to the boat and start to grow. We do have very good anti-foul paint to stop this and it makes it easier to remove them, but they will continue to gather on the boat and require scraping off for the rest of the voyage. To do this we get into the sea wearing a diving mask so that we can see underwater well enough to scrape them off. Hope that helps.

Ship's Log

Today the sea has been lumpy with some big waves. Confused patterns of waves have made it difficult to row. We were just working to make the boat face the right way as we were blown by the wind. During the afternoon the waves were smaller and the rowing became easier as we kept up the two nautical miles per hour pace. We are both tired today, not really having had an easy day. We always enjoy our evening meal together and our spirits are lifted in the afternoon, reading our messages. The cabin has been too hot for me and during the writing of the blog I think it has made me feel out of sorts, although we were both more upbeat at 8pm this evening.

James thinks that there may have been a small shark near the boat overnight. The AIS alerted us to a cargo ship called 'Oreanica'. We saw the boat on the horizon, on a parallel course, but heading in the opposite direction, so all was clear. We had another long spell of rain; James was at the oars again! As it went dark, we enjoyed looking at a beautiful crescent moon together.

10th February 2010

Beech Boys' Blog

The power of chicken tikka and email! Overall yesterday was a difficult day in the ocean rowing office! We both found ourselves lacking in energy, maybe still not in the routine of rowing at night-time after the week on para-anchor? So we were pleased to keep the boat moving well despite the feelings of weariness. Then as the afternoon progressed James read out all our latest emails and as usual this gave us a real boost and brought a few laughs. The evening meal was one of our favourite dehydrated ones - chicken tikka! As we have a shift change at 7.30pm our evening meals fall either side of this. James eats at about 7pm and I eat at 7.30pm. It is often the best bit of the day as we chat, eat and watch the sunset. Thanks to everyone praying for our energy levels and sleep - we are feeling more refreshed today.

As in all classic crime thrillers, someone will be in a car and realise they are being 'tailed', usually resulting in a high speed chase to lose the car which is following. Overnight James thought his head torch beam had picked out a big fish beside the boat. This morning as we changed shift there was a splash or two from behind the boat. On investigation we saw a large fish following precisely behind the rudder, and every so often it gave it a nudge! As I went on oars I felt the foot steering plate, which controls the rudder position, being shaken by the fish. We thought it must be trying to bite it, or nudge it, as there was a lot of splashing from the stern of

'Beech Boys'. Over the next two hours our 'high speed' chase to lose the fish began. Various evasive manoeuvres were tried - zigzagging, doubling back, handbrake turning (surprised us too, as we didn't know we had a handbrake!) and finally pretending to be completely uninterested and too grown up to be worried by such matters. Thankfully the latter proved successful and we haven't had any more problems. It will be interesting to look at the rudder next time we clean the boat to see if there are any marks on it!

It would be good to hear if anyone can identify our mystery fish. Here is our 'identi-fish' summary. Length: five to six feet, colour: brown, blue, green with mottled pattern on sides. Long dorsal fin which tapers to a fine point, 'boomerang' shaped tail also tapering to fine points, lateral fins quite wide and triangular. Overall it looked 'shark' like, but it would be interesting to hear from anyone being able to tell us more definitely from this description what it is! May have a few fin prints to add to this later once we have looked at the rudder.

Thanks to Katie and Hannah for telling us the dolphins we saw recently were Atlantic Spotted Dolphins. We haven't seen any since then, but it is good to know their name!

We are pleased to see we have only 1,500 nautical miles to go. We keep ticking them off as fast as we can!

<u>Ship's Log</u>

We did some clothes washing today, then wore them while still wet to dry them and keep us cool. We had the rear cabin hatch open as it was calm. It was nice to rest in the cabin out of the sun. Over the last 24 hours to 1.30pm we have covered 50 miles - now we just have to keep this up!

11th February 2010

Beech Boys' Blog

Last night we discovered that some of the kit by the main cabin hatch looked wet. This was surprising as it had been hot and dry all day. In trying to discover the source of the water James thought it was coming from the fire blanket which is mounted in a case on the bulkhead. Although there was something dripping from the fire blanket case the actual source of the liquid was the bulkhead compass mounted above it! For some reason this compass, which is like a clear sphere with a compass card mounted inside it and filled with special oil, was leaking. The sphere is now half full of oil and the compass still works, but why this should have happened is a mystery. We both use this compass to steer the right course, as we look towards it from our rowing position. The GPS repeater system provides a digital compass display which is still working and visible from the rowing position, but it is good to be able to look at both. We cannot do much to repair this so we shall just have to monitor it for the time being. Rather like the compass in 'Pirates of the Caribbean', which took them to the place their heart most wanted to visit, we will be content with it doing that whether full of oil or not.

On our 9.30am shift change, the rain started again so I had a soggy time at the oars, as the rain was falling very steadily. At last James got a break from the heavy cloud bursts! Eventually the sun burst through a broken patch of cloud to the south of us and from 11.30am there was an ongoing improvement. The large rain clouds passed by and more blue sky emerged. We still have a cloud mass upwind of our position, so possibly further rain later. At least for the moment we can get some clothes dried in the warm sun. Over the last 24 hours, winds have fallen light, so our progress has dropped a little. By 1.30pm today it looks as though we will have covered around 47 miles since 1.30pm yesterday. Our target for each day is 50 nautical miles, so not far off the pace.

No further appearances of the unidentified fish which followed us yesterday. Food highlights today were a large pack of KP peanuts and some boiled sweets!

News on Joe going to the disco to come tomorrow - incredible!

<u>Ship's Log</u>

The combination of rain and sun has meant we have seen a number of partial rainbows. At the end of the day some big rain clouds have been picked out by the setting sun, turning them red and mauve. Hopefully it will not be wet again overnight. The rain clouds reminded us of cartoon comedy clouds. They were dark, rounded and fairly low to the horizon. You could see rain falling out of the bottom of the cloud and if they moved overhead you got absolutely soaked!

The evening wind has now died right off and in the calm sea the boat speed has dropped off. Heavy showers have passed on either side of us.

12th February 2010

Beech Boys' Blog

The mixed bag of weather yesterday was made more memorable by the visit of five or six whales! At 3pm, as I was rowing I noticed the dorsal fin and black back of a whale surface 50 metres behind the boat and I called to James to grab the camera. As he emerged from the cabin we both realised there was more than one and they had surrounded us. Then a fish flew five or six feet out of the water followed by a whale! This happened several times and the whale seemed to be throwing the fish around. As the whales stayed close around 'Beech Boys', passing underneath the bow and stern and turning tightly this way and that we were starting to be puzzled and a little worried as to their intentions. It then became clear that the fish they were after were using 'Beech Boys' as a cover in a deadly game of Hide and Seek!

Visiting Whale - false killer

One of the whales positioned itself directly under the boat and we could hear its sonar type call. This stopped the fish dodging under the boat and the whales then took it in turns to go for the fish. As we looked over the side, we could see a fish swimming next to us one second, only to be snapped up by a whale, leaving particles of fish remains in the water. They were with us for about 30 minutes and although it was extraordinary to witness we were glad when their dinner party finished and they moved on. Unfortunately our video camera did not record the action, but we got a few close-up stills of the whales next to the boat. The whales were 20 feet long, black in colour, with lighter grey under the belly, rounded/blunt nose, keen on chasing and eating fish! We wondered what type of whale they were.

The other interesting story of the day relates to Joe the Swimmer. Every so often he has had a fish ask him what he is doing and he has now built up a following within the fish world. Joe was asking them about the phosphorescence in the water at night-time, which is like patches of bright light appearing in random places on the water's surface. Apparently this is generated from the dance floor of the underwater disco! John Travolta danced on a colour flashing disco floor in 'Saturday Night Fever' and this is their ocean disco equivalent! The big event this weekend is the 'Bop until you Drop Disco!' with some great live artistes and amazingly Joe has been given a ticket! Apparently Hake That, Tuna Turner, Gulls Aloud, Kylie Minnow and a Shellfish Presley tribute act will all be performing. It's a hot ticket! We will let you know how Joe gets on after the weekend.

A quick mention of Yellow Jelly Baby. No one knows her real name, but apparently her stage name is Bubbles.

<u>Ship's Log</u>

The southeasterly wind seemed OK at first, but it changed through south to southwest making a very slow afternoon. We put waterproof putty on the compass to stop the oil leaking out. There were rain showers at 7.30pm which meant that our change-over on rowing shifts were very wet. It was slow, hard rowing. James rowed for one and a half hours in heavy rain, and with the wind as it was, only made 0.5 knots an hour, but it was a great effort. Winds continued from the south-west as we rowed into the evening. James was brilliant at getting me organised with the course to row on, as I was having difficulty with my glasses seeing the compass and GPS repeater with it being so cloudy and therefore no stars to work from.

13th and 14th February 2010

Beech Boys' Blog

Late Friday afternoon the wind turned to the south and eventually overnight became south-westerly which really slowed progress. We were rowing across the waves, which in the dark also slows you up as you can't position the boat to deal with them so well. Some of waves hitting the side of the boat had enough force to send you falling sideways off the seat!

Saturday 13th - we were rowing against a westerly and losing the battle. We kept rowing, making 3 nautical miles of progress through the whole of the night. It was then 189 nautical miles to our next waypoint, at 19 degrees north, 40 degrees west. With the wind directly from the west we went on para-anchor at 7.30am, after only fractions of a mile gained in the previous hour of rowing. We both got into the cabin to get some sleep. The forecast was indicating a return to north-easterly winds within 24 hours, so we made the best use of the day to rest, clean the hull, and have a spa treatment. What luxury! A fresh Atlantic sea water plunge, followed by a sponge down with fresh water in a yellow bucket to remove the salt, before letting the heat of the sun dry our skin. You really feel refreshed after such pampering!

Joe went to the 'Bop until You Drop Disco' which he said was quite an experience. When was the last time you saw an octopus breakdancing?! Afterwards, because everyone knew he was doing the Atlantic swim, he had the good fortune to be invited backstage to meet Gulls Aloud. However, having not managed to get a ticket for Bubbles to get into the disco with him, news of this was met with a frosty silence from Bubbles. It's going to be a tense Valentine's Day here on the boat tomorrow - we hope he has got Bubbles a card!

Ship's Log

James set the alarm for 10.30am and we checked the wind direction, but there was no change. At 11.30am it was still a westerly and a little bit stronger. Faced with this we decided that all we could do was to remain on the para-anchor. Custard in today's food bag made a refreshing change. Some of it went into the leftover syrup pudding for me. James decided to have it on its own - a bit of a drink really, but very nice!

It is really frustrating to be stuck again - going nowhere. Psalm 40:1 'Trust and wait patiently on the Lord'. We get as much rest as we can so that we are ready to go for it when the wind improves. The winds should go to the north north-east tomorrow, so while we stay on para-anchor, James will clean the hull and I will repack the front cabin. The wind continues steady from the west, although there are no big waves, it will be impossible to make progress today.

At 8.30pm, we had drifted back five miles on our morning position, so 194 miles to the next waypoint. James had a bar of emergency chocolate from his girlfriend Laura's family - it really did say 'Emergency Chocolate' on the wrapper! We ate that during the day. We also used some of the hot chocolate powder to make up some chocoshakes. Chocolate counts for a lot at times like this!

We phoned Emily Robinson, from Derby today. She had won a picture competition that we had organised, and the prize had been to receive a phone call from us on Christmas Day. However, as we had ended up being at home on Christmas, we had decided to ring her mid-ocean. Unfortunately she was not at home and we ended up speaking to her dad who was pleased to hear from us! We rang my brother Eric, and his wife Jill and their children Lauren and Max. They sang Happy Birthday to James over the phone and gave us a really big cheer for doing so well, which was really encouraging. Eric thought James' interview on Border TV had gone extremely well. It was a lovely sunset, and the wind had started to go north, so we decided to go to bed and check the situation again at 3am.

Sunday 14th - we checked the wind direction every few hours overnight. This seemed a lot of work. It always felt easier to stay asleep than crawl out of the cabin and see what was going on, but we wanted to get going as soon as we could. The wind was gradually turning to the north. We decided that we would come off the para-anchor when it was at least

30 degrees. In the end this was at first light and although we would be rowing across the waves for a while the wind was continuing to turn easterly. Rowing across both wind and waves for the day is not given to rapid progress, but we started to slowly reclaim the seven miles we had drifted east while on para-anchor. Amazingly we had dolphins with us from 10am until sunset! They varied in number and there seemed to be different pods. We enjoyed watching them alongside us, or behind the boat. Every so often one would turn onto its back to show a pink and white underbelly as it splashed its tail, doing a dolphin backstroke. We weren't sure, but they may have been eating fish when they did this, however for whatever reason it was amusing to watch as they cruised alongside and we were able to hear their high pitch calls. It would be interesting to know what they meant! Probably "Row faster, row faster!" They have been good company and their presence with us has helped ease the time on the oars. James got some great underwater video, which we had fun viewing on the laptop.

Joe had a card for Bubbles, so a happier atmosphere has returned! We just don't mention discos or Gulls Aloud at the moment!

James phoned Christine. Her mum and sister Pauline were visiting her in Coniston, so we were able to chat to them too which was good. Pauline is a physiotherapist so I was able to ask her about my hand. I had been sleeping with my fingers in a plastic case to try and keep them straight, which seemed to be helping. We plan to phone Christine again on James' birthday on 17th February. It has been odd to be away from each other on Valentine's Day. It hasn't rained tonight, which is the first time in quite a while.

15th February 2010

Beech Boys' Blog

In the early hours of this morning we had a favourable wind shift to give us an easterly. So with the following sea as well we should make good some of the time lost on our para-anchor holiday! James invented a new game last night - satellite soccer! You use two of the stars as goalposts and whenever a satellite goes between the stars you score a goal! In a close contest last night I won 1-0, although James did have a satellite just past the post. If any of the games go to penalties, it could take a long time to get a result! We may add in meteors as another means to score a goal and try it out tonight. All being well we will have a cloudless night sky.

The bulkhead compass that was leaking oil has now been 'fixed' as far as we are able to repair it. We couldn't identify the leak point and decided to use some Araldite sealing putty to cover the side of the globe we view from inside the cabin. This seems to have done the job and provides us with a useable bulkhead compass. Although the compass card does spin around very quickly at times!

As we focus on making progress westward we are all too aware how dependant we are on the weather. Emotions can change quickly from one part of the day to the next depending on how the wind and waves are treating us and whether we are rowing in the rain, or baking in the sun! Some more days with a following breeze will certainly be encouraging, as the 'miles to go' figure ticks down just that little bit quicker!

Ship's Log

It was sunny and hot through to 3pm, then after this an extensive cloud cooled the afternoon. We were both able to sleep in the cabin during the day, with the stern hatch open as the waves were smaller. We decided to keep with our 'Go -West' plan for the next few days, and get across longitude, 40 degrees west - a good milestone to aim for. We took out the centreboard as there was a following wind, and this helped with our boat speed.

We found Christmas stuff today, and will open it on James' birthday. All our 6 Nations Rugby international result predictions were right, although not the scorelines! Our friend Jill Birch has been in touch to tell us that she thinks the whales we saw were 'False Killers'! The overnight satellite football game that we started ended in a no-score draw.

16th February 2010

Beech Boys' Blog

We have had some useful tailwinds which have improved progress over the last 24 hours for which we are grateful. Overnight the wonderful display of stars became enveloped in cloud. It is interesting to watch the darker shade of black cloud cross the sky and extinguish the stars. Sometimes it is temporary and sometimes a glimmer from the brighter stars can still be seen through the cloud. In the few hours to sunrise it was total cloud cover and as we have progressed this morning it has again been under an overcast sky. We will have to be careful with our power use today, as there will be less sunlight on the solar panels to recharge the batteries. We did some further barnacle clearing yesterday afternoon. It is surprising how much can attach itself, but a day stationary on the para-anchor will not have helped.

Following Joe the Swimmer's disastrous visit to the disco he has tried to make things up to Bubbles. He asked us yesterday if he could use the satellite phone to call Bunches internet florist to get some flowers for her. Commendable thinking, but we had to explain to Joe that Bunches' excellent delivery service did not yet extend to mid-ocean delivery. So 'Plan B' was hatched and by consulting the reference book, 'How To Make Anything Out Of Paper - The Concise Version' written by Crease and Fold, a bunch of paper flowers was soon created. By careful use of striped toothpaste we were able to create some stunning patterns on the petals - they looked amazing. Bubbles was delighted to receive them, but some of the success of the paper flower gift was lost as she insisted on putting them in water! All you can say is "It is the thought that counts!" on these occasions.

The big culinary challenge is on tonight as we tackle Shrove Tuesday on-board 'Beech Boys' with our own pancake party.

In La Gomera we purchased a pancake mix. On the packet the words 'con todos los ingredients necesarios' suggest nothing else is needed, which we hope is true! Our lack of ability in understanding the Spanish instructions on the packet has forced us to invent our own! Since we lost the cooker lid, which doubled as a small frying pan, we will try to create a sort of scone in the bottom of the main pan rather than a typical thin pancake. News on how we get on tomorrow! We do have lots of maple syrup with which to offset any deficiencies we may have in other departments of pancake making!

Ship's Log

It has been cloudy all day, but no rain and the temperatures have been pleasant. Northeasterly winds about 5 knots. We watched the Storm Petrel pecking things off the water surface as it walked/paddled along with its feet, all very delicate and precise. The overcast conditions meant we had to take care with the batteries today, as both are only at 70% capacity. We switched off the AIS and GPS in the afternoon to save batteries and to ensure we can use these overnight. We ran the watermaker briefly to produce 1.5 litres which should see us through until tomorrow. The evening pancake party was a massive boost to morale! We managed the complicated task of adding the correct amount of water to the pancake mix and made six superb pancakes. They had a delicate flavour of peanut from the peanut butter oil we used and with a great dollop of syrup on top were soon snaffled up! To quote

James, who tried out the first one, “It doesn’t taste like anything else we have eaten in a while!” It was a bit of a fiddle, but we had a great time as we took it in turns to eat one, row the boat and watch the sunset. Once the sun had set we looked on in wonder at the crescent moon. Again we could see the very faint outline of the full moon. Apologies now if you ever eat pancakes with us in the future, as we will probably say, “Do you remember that time when we were ....”

17th February 2010

Beech Boys’ Blog

James’ 19th birthday

Day 44 at sea and a celebratory mood aboard ‘Beech Boys’ today as James had his 19th birthday at sea! When we changed over our rowing shift at 1.30am, I sang 'Happy Birthday' to him. No let up from rowing, but we had a few presents from Christmas on-board which were opened today at 11am. Sandra Hoving's present turned out to be a harmonica, so we now have two on-board. I had given James a kazoo as a present, so there are now plenty of musical opportunities! James also had some bags of chocolate gold coins, a party popper, crackers, balloons and sparklers to make the event that little more memorable! More of Grandma's Christmas cake to serve as birthday cake too - fantastic! We both went for a swim. James enjoyed his birthday swim, with his cake in a bowl with sparklers stuck into it, and wearing a party hat. But we couldn't get the sparklers to light! Good messages on email for James' birthday, and a great poem about the row from Andy Adamson from Cool Pilates. There were nice cards from Norman and Pauline Murray, and Christine which we had taken on-board with us. James phoned Lydia, Mum and Laura for birthday chats.

We also had some classic party games. Musical chairs - after two hours the music stops and you change seats and if you find yourself in the rowing seat you row until the music stops - in two hours time! Pass the parcel - it only had one wrapper so I had to fix it to make sure James got to undo the wrapping. Hide and seek - we had limited success with this, even counting to 100 didn't really create enough time to find a good place to hide! We will catch up with emails later today, so if you sent James birthday greetings - thank you for remembering!

We also celebrated passing the halfway point today - hurray! Good to have reached this milestone. The winds and currents should become more favourable to us now, with the expected result that we should complete the second half a bit quicker. Christine told us that Simon Chalk in his Woodvale Challenge update has predicted that we will finish on Day 73, based on our current progress. Our own thoughts when we started the crossing were that it would take us 60 to 65 days, so we are outside of this, but given that we have had nearly 10 days on para-anchor we are probably on track with our pacing.

We can report a new record in consecutive fish jumps. This had stood at five until this morning when a new record of six was established. This was a Dorado, not a flying fish. It reminded us a bit of the triple jump in athletics.

<u>Ship's Log</u>

All our compasses seem to be slightly different, which has puzzled us for a while, until we remembered that the GPS repeater is a magnetic bearing, rather than a true bearing. We checked with Christine and she confirms our 1pm position, using the Woodvale website, which was helpful and now we're all happy again with our navigation! There is hard work ahead if we are going to make the Woodvale prediction of 73 days! It has been a lovely day with a great sunrise and sunset; it has been hot with a helpful but gentle wind. A birthday to remember - when we passed the halfway point!

Evening sunshine

18th February 2010

Beech Boys' Blog

The birthday celebrations yesterday were a definite highlight of the voyage so far. As it was particularly hot in the afternoon we both went for a swim in the deep end - over 5,000m deep. We tried but we couldn't touch the bottom! The water was very clear and you could see a fair distance, making it easy to watch a few of the fish that escort us along.

The last couple of nights we have had a crescent moon. It isn't above the horizon for long, but its elegant presence in the night sky is incredibly beautiful. We know many people have said they think of us when they see the moon, so it was an encouraging reminder of all those people thinking about us.

The main batteries we have on 'Beech Boys' were supplied by Exide. The solar panels recharge them each day and we monitor our use of them to keep them in good condition. The very cloudy day of 16th February meant we needed to be more careful, as less charge was going to be put back into them from the solar panels. The laptop computer, iPod and satellite phone all need recharging every so often, so making good choices about when to do this enables the demands being made on the batteries to be spread out. We are really pleased with how the power system of panels and batteries is working. It is a great relief not to have to be continually trouble shooting problems with the electrical equipment.

Wildlife recently seen - a large bird with white plumage, long beak and a very long forked tail. Graceful in flight it did a couple of laps of 'Beech Boys' before heading off elsewhere.

Looks as though today will be hot; with very little cloud there is no respite from the sun when rowing. Shirts dunked in water are proving an aid to keeping cool, along with brimmed hats and sunglasses. Again a light following breeze should help move us closer to Antigua.

Ship's Log

Overnight the wind turned to the north, so it was blowing across the boat, and eventually in the second half of the night became a north-easterly. It's a good following breeze of 5 to 10 knots. At 1.30pm a Grimaldi Line container ship passed a mile astern of us heading north. We are both aware we want to get some good miles in, so a lot depends on how well we row each night, as well as the wind direction and our ability to concentrate and keep a good boat speed. We should cross 40 degrees west by early morning of 19th February. Targeting 50 degrees west next! We enjoyed golden syrup with our tinned pineapple at teatime - it tasted great! One of James' birthday presents from Laura was a message in a bottle set, which he launched overboard at 18°43'N, 39°40W. Will it ever be found?

19th February 2010

Beech Boys' Blog

A pretty good day yesterday for eating up some of the miles we still have to row. No crosswinds overnight, but it has gone from being a gentle to a very light/occasional breeze as we go through Friday morning. Boat speed has slowed a little as a result. Yesterday with the slight sea we were able to have the stern cabin hatch open so sleeping in the afternoon was easier as the cabin had a through breeze. In fact, for once it was possible to have two different temperature zones - very hot on deck at the oars and if you stay long enough to be cooled by the draft a 'colder' cabin area for snoozing. Refreshing.

Increasingly we are experiencing the strange 'gravitational' effects present in the cabin at night time. We are still investigating, but think it is linked to the alarm clock. Whenever the alarm goes off the person woken up by it experiences additional gravitational forces, making it very difficult to get up from the very comfortable mattress supplied to us by Goacher Sails. This makes tasks like sitting up to put a shirt on extremely tiring. Frequently having made the effort to do such a thing the person is instantly asleep again, the exertion having clearly exhausted them. Everyday tasks, such as putting shoes on, take three times as long as normal! The only known antidote to this peculiar condition is about 15 minutes on the oars, with the iPod turned up loud!

We are pleased to have now passed 40 degrees longitude west. Our next target is to reach 50 degrees west, so our compass course will be pretty much the same for the rest of the month as we track westward! It will take us to the beginning of March to reach this point, but after that it will seem as though we are at least getting 'close' to our target of Antigua.

Ship's Log

Gentle easterly wind gradually died out by 11am. It had been very cloudy up until then, when suddenly it became very hot and sunny, with no cloud or wind. It was very hard rowing in this heat, making 1.5 knots. We were going forward, but having to pace it carefully in such high temperatures. We experimented with making our compact emergency ration (which looks like a block of shortbread, and is designed to produce a high energy food-mix) into a dessert - mixing it with some water, and then adding golden syrup, it tastes very similar to the semolina and honey we had for dessert recently. James cooled off with a swim and cleaned some barnacles off the boat. I managed to accidentally hit a fish that was jumping out of the water with my oar last night - it jumped out of the water a further time after the collision, so hopefully that meant it was OK! I made a new seat pad from some foam taken from the small cabin cushion; it's an improvement to the original one we had which is now rather flattened! It has been very slow rowing overnight. We are both finding it hard to wake up and get going at changeover time, managing 1 to 1.5 knots at night, but not really the speeds we were hoping for at this stage.

20th and 21st February 2010

Beech Boys' Blog

Light winds, or no wind and calm sea, are the order of the day at the moment. It is certainly preferable to being stuck on para-anchor, but progress is considerably slowed. We continue to be positive, as we aim to row as well as we can in the conditions we have each day. It would be brilliant to have some steady easterly winds for the rest of the voyage. Currently the forecast for the next five days suggests that these light conditions will continue. Whenever the sea is calm we change from rowing with our macon oars to the cleaver blades. These are slightly longer oars and give more power, however once any crosswinds set in we have to change back, as the motion of the boat makes each stroke awkward and ineffective, as the blades catch on the waves.

Bubbles had a narrow escape yesterday. She and Joe had gone on to the front cabin roof to watch the sunset. Bubbles decided to do the Kate Winslet Titanic pose, lost her balance and fell in! Joe dived in after her and kept her afloat. Fortunately, James was eating his evening meal and quickly scooped them up with a bucket, which was just as well as Bubbles' sugar coating had attracted unwanted attention. As James scooped them up, a large fish crashed against the outside of the bucket. It was not pleased since its next meal had disappeared before its eyes and been replaced with a large yellow bucket, which didn't feel or taste good as he bashed into it. As we said afterwards, "It was better the fish hitting the bucket than Bubbles kicking the bucket!"

Ship's Log - 20th February

Early morning was peaceful on the ocean, with no wind, just a slight swell. The sun was behind some cloud, so the hotter temperatures were held back temporarily.

We had been praying for our family. We were so thankful for their unrelenting support and encouragement. It encouraged us to find the best in ourselves for each day. We also prayed about the rest of the row that lay ahead. It would be good to complete it and have a holiday. Isaiah 40:31 'But they who wait for the Lord will renew their strength, they will run and not be weary', a favourite Bible verse, helped us to bring our thoughts and concerns over the time ahead back to Jesus.

It was very hot today. The wind was very light and variable, sometimes from the side, from behind us, or for variety from ahead of us! As the sun set the sea was very glassy, and I used the cleaver blades for a while. A southerly wind blew across us after 12.30pm, it was only light, but made rowing awkward with the cleaver blades. The shape of the cleavers means it only takes a small wavelet to catch the bottom edge. The drag on the blade as it is recovered is very disruptive to your rhythm. It is all too easy to keep bashing your legs with the oar handles. It seemed to be a very slow, frustrating few miles, although it was good to enjoy the peacefulness of the ocean. The crystal clear ocean is aquarium-like. The clarity of the water and the view it affords us of the fish is terrific. My left hand was quite sore today and it was difficult restarting each rowing session.

We are aiming for an arrival time of around the 14th March in Antigua. It will be a challenge to get there by then. We keep praying for helpful weather conditions, but are very conscious that the world does not revolve entirely around us. Hebrews 11:1, 'Faith is being sure of what we hope for, certain of what we do not see'. We are challenged to have the faith and self-belief to keep going. Faith that we can do it, to keep rowing night and day, certain that we will reach an island we cannot yet see!

Ship's Log - 21st February

After sunrise it was cloudy until 11am again, and then extremely hot and sunny. The sea was very calm from 9.30 until 12.00 noon. After lunch we rowed into a westerly, which was a headwind. It was slow work and the boat was jiggled uncomfortably by the waves hitting the side, it was not brilliant! We felt a bit low this afternoon with the delay this has all brought to our progress. It is teaching me patience, to trust God and believe it will improve, that we will get to Antigua and in good time. It was lovely to speak to Christine on the phone. Our telephone link-up with Bob Ketts from Furness Plastics, who was cruising on the 'Oriana' didn't succeed. We will try again tomorrow at 7.30pm.

James keeps going steadily and is positive, which is fantastic. It was lovely talking together over the mealtime this evening. It is always a part of the day we look forward to and tonight we had butterscotch Angel Delight. We are trying to make progress to the southwest to see if we can get better wind direction over the next few days. Overnight it was calm and the light wind gradually turned to the east. At 1am I heard a whale. The impressive sound of its explosive exhalation penetrated the darkness as it appeared on the surface near to 'Beech Boys'. It gave the impression of being a reasonable size judging by the noise of its breathing and the phosphorescence that its shape made as it broke the surface. After the very close encounter we had previously had with whales it was a relief that it stayed its distance! It is quite incredible experiencing such events. In everyday life there are whales coming onto the ocean's surface to breathe, but we just don't have the opportunity to see them and have personal contact with them. To be out here and to have these encounters is a total privilege and a wonder. The noise of the whale's sonar clicks is very audible. It stayed around for about 20 minutes, but even using the torch to shine into the dark, I could not see it properly. It was awe-inspiring, a bit eerie and slightly scary all at the same time. A totally magnificent ocean moment!

22nd February 2010

Beech Boys' Blog

We have spent the last few days in the classroom of patience and perseverance! Our forward progress slowed by light winds and odd currents has been frustrating and we have had to learn to cope with a different scenario to the one we wanted. Instead of the 'miles to go' figure declining at a steady rate and having the encouragement of seeing such positive progress we were grafting in the heat to make, well, not much progress at all! As we row we can view 'Beech Boys' boat speed on our instrument display. In the afternoon rowing into the wind our speed through the water was stuck on 0.0 knots. As we watched the instrument panel, hoping to see the good news that our rowing was gaining us ground towards Antigua we just had to dig deep, as we were continually confronted with the zeroes on the display. Our approach was that some progress was better than none, however as you pulled on the oars it was a mental battle not to give in. At one point it took 1.5 hours at 'full speed' to do one nautical mile!

We have worked hard to keep our spirits up. This has been achieved with the subtle use of as many motivational tools as we could think of! Extra food treats, a joke and trivia question card pack, discussions on our top five book titles, satellite phone calls home to Christine and a butterscotch Angel Delight at teatime! Overnight we decided to row southwest with the aim of finding an improvement in conditions. Prayers for more favourable winds were answered as the overnight calm gave way to a gentle breeze from the east which is now a southeasterly on Monday morning. We can row off this and make progress west which is much better! We are now covering over two nautical miles each hour - yippee!

A fabulous orange band spread across the horizon at sunset on Sunday. This wonderful curtain of orange gradually dissolved into the evening to provide a completely clear sky. A brilliant display of stars produced the 'wow' factor as we looked up into the dome of night which engulfed us. The drama of shooting stars proved to be an added bonus.

Typical sunset

Ship's Log

No cloud, just the 'hot dial' turned up a long way! Batteries are all charging well, which is good for making water and having drinks. We have been able to have the stern hatch open otherwise it would be too hot to rest in the cabin. The afternoon winds are from the south, blowing across the boat and slowing progress. By the evening the wind had gone light. We aim to head southwest in the hope of finding more easterly wind. Overall it has been a more encouraging day.

AIS picked up contact with 'Sian C' at 9pm. She was travelling northeast and we saw her on the horizon; with her lights on she was easy to see about three miles away. Seeing her broadside on made it a straightforward task to decide there was no need for a course change. We put the VHF on, but heard nothing and did not try to call them.

Position at 8.30pm: 18°29'N, 41°38'W

23rd February 2010

Beech Boys' Blog

The BIG milestone of 50 days at sea should click through at 1.30pm today. It is strange looking back to preparations in La Gomera - they all seem a very, very long time ago now!

Monday afternoon took us back to a southerly wind, so a bit more rowing across the waves. This morning we had a better direction again with enough east in it to improve our speed. We are keen to get further south toward 18 degrees north. Our plan was to do this gradually, but we are not making much progress with this of late, as the winds have been from the southeast. If we get a return to a very calm sea, or a northeasterly we will be aiming to drop down, as we think the winds will be less variable there than we have been experiencing. Obviously it takes a long time to alter your position to any great extent when you are powered by oars. It is therefore quite possible that by the time you have rowed to where the weather has previously been advantageous, because of the time delay to row to that point it is no longer there! In an effort to relocate to a more favoured point on the ocean you have the real possibility of having to face either frustration and disappointment or the euphoria of winning the weather lottery.

Our current focus is to push on through the '1,000 miles to go' mark. The 50 degree longitude line is now only 460 miles away. It will begin to feel like the home straight after that! It is interesting monitoring our emotions. We have found that whenever we are making good speed in the right direction tiredness seems to diminish and our morale remains high with little, or no effort. Days when we have lost ground through trickier conditions have a greater impact on our morale and how tired we feel. At this stage we are finding there can be a very thin dividing line between feeling fine and feeling low. Every so often we do some "How do you feel?" checks. These are scored on a scale of 1 to 10 and cover a variety of areas e.g. tiredness, energy levels, motivation for the day. It often helps to talk about these things and we can help each other along. A massive boost for us continues to be the messages that we pick up on email and our phone calls home. Where would we be without these? We are so thankful for all those people sending them to us!

Breakfast today was a little odd. Tucking into mint flavoured porridge was a surprise! Unfortunately when packaging all the breakfasts several months ago we had run out of heavy duty plastic bags, so some porridge was packed in normal food bags. The aroma of Kendal Mint Cake in today's food bag has permeated the plastic and given the porridge a new minty taste. After trying to eat a bowl of this we don't think there will be a rush for mint flavoured porridge as an extension to the oat cereal breakfast range currently available in the supermarkets!

Ship's Log

Overnight progress was slow as we dealt with crosswinds. They were not strong, but enough to upset our rhythm, and were sometimes more of a headwind than a crosswind. Remembering Isaiah 41:10: 'Fear not for I am with you', it is good to know that God is with us. We pray for guidance with our route choice whether to head south or hold the line and gradually ease south. In the end we decided to stick with it and go south gradually. We will use wind shifts to get south if they occur, or go that way if it is calm. It is a lovely sunny day, and the wind is turning from a side wind to be on the stern quarter which is a tremendous blessing. Thank you Lord! I have found the last few days hard, with emotions going up and down as a result of the weather conditions we have experienced. I want to push on with the row and not miss time with Christine and our family friend Caroline in Antigua. I don't want it to be a waste of time for them with no one to welcome home! We had a great food parcel today - vegetable curry boil-in-the-bag and chicken tikka, with butterscotch Angel Delight for afters!

Overall we made better progress today which is encouraging and builds hope of a speedier conclusion to the row. Christine sent emails through to us, as she does every day. Since the Woodvale Race site had not been updated recently we had loads to read which was nice. James is always so good at reading them out. We received one about a round Britain rowing race being held this summer. We both decided we were not interested!

We continue to trust we will have better conditions. It all seems very variable for all the boat crews at the moment. Jeremiah 32:17: 'Nothing is too difficult for you'. We prayed together for more favourable winds.

Position at 9.30pm: 18°29'N, 42°8'W

24th February 2010

Beech Boys' Blog

Before we began the row, one of the things people often commented on was, "It will all look the same" and "Won't you find it boring?", which are perfectly fair assumptions! Well even after 50 days at sea there is always something that comes along to surprise you!

As you row you have your back to the direction of travel, so effectively you are always looking at where you were, rather than where you are going. As there are few obstacles to avoid out here that is fine and you steer your course by checking the boat's heading on the GPS display in front of you. It was therefore with some surprise yesterday that as I looked up from the GPS display I noticed a green object about 75 metres behind 'Beech Boys'. After a moment or two of consideration as to what this was, it became apparent that it was an inflatable green crocodile which needed some re-inflation! It would have been fun to have a photo of the crocodile, but it would have meant retracing our steps and rowing into the wind - which did not appeal! Suddenly my mind was full of questions. Where did it come from? Was anyone upset they had lost it? Should I have rowed back against the wind to rescue it? If we rescued it, what would we do with it? Was there a reward for finding it?

While answers to these questions were being pondered, we were getting ready for the 3.30pm shift change. Simultaneously we both said "What is that?" as we noticed a number of objects floating either side of 'Beech Boys'. A colander type bucket, a plastic plant pot, a bucket and some non-descript debris! Instantly we grasped the importance of this flotsam - there must be a garden centre ahead! Thoughts of whether it would have a cafeteria and the prospect of tea and cake loomed large in our minds! Bubbles was keen to buy a few bits to create a roof garden on the front cabin, while Joe wondered if he could buy a water feature for the boat. Why this should be necessary when we are surrounded by such a huge oceanic water feature we didn't understand!

After several hours looking for signs to the garden centre we realised we must have missed them and had to downscale our aspirations for tea and scones to a sports energy drink and a handful of sultanas. At least it goes to show there is more going on out on the ocean than you might realise!

It was brilliant to speak last night to Bob Ketts, from Furness Plastics, who is holidaying on the cruise liner 'Oriana'. It had taken them five days to cross from Maderia to St Lucia. We were only a little envious as we continued to progress at a more sedate pace!

Ship's Log

Some overnight speed with following waves and wind, but from 5.30am it was slow and then slower! Southwest-westerly winds made for a hard day of rowing in hot sunshine. We have to put this to one side and get on with the next two hour shift, the next night-time and the next day's rowing. Unfortunately the forecast is not any different for the following few days. We trust God will help us to stay positive through it all.

We had a clothes and body wash to help freshen ourselves up.

Position at 8pm: 18°31'N, 42°40'W

25th February 2010

Beech Boys' Blog

Somewhat unintentionally we have created a new activity for anyone visiting the Woodvale Atlantic Rowing Race website. It's called 'Spot the Difference' and involves looking at yesterday's and today's 'Beech Boys' green dot position. Very simply, you then have to see if you can spot the difference! Nine out of ten people say they can 'spot the difference' and that we have moved forward, but it takes careful examination to notice this.

Why the slower progress? It would be all too easy to put this down to a lack of favourable wind and the heat of the day sapping energy levels. However, we have to come clean and say we have lost the remote control! We suspect the slow motion button has been accidentally pressed and until we can reset the remote, similar slow progress looks likely. We have looked in all the usual places - behind the cushions, down the back of the sofa, but nothing! We are not sure how far reaching the slow motion effect is, but we know other boats are having some similar slowing of progress. In fact you may find it takes you longer than normal to read this blog, as we don't actually know how far the slow motion influence has spread. At least we haven't gone to super slow-mo!

Needless to say it is a challenge to one's resolve. What seemed a fairly straightforward task to break through the '1,000 miles to go' barrier has become a more elusive one with another 83 nautical miles to go before we cross that point. To add insult to injury progress had decreased to the extent that we were issued with a parking ticket yesterday! We have a few days to appeal, but we could do without this. As always looking on the bright side at least we weren't oar clamped and fortunately we don't have Donkey from 'Shrek' asking, "Are we nearly there yet?"

Now to some rather exciting, breaking news. This morning we discovered the snacks bag from Day 48. Mysteriously it had somehow been repacked in the wrong locker. So extra chocolate rations today - hurray!

Ship's Log

Today we received a message from Christine. Zena, my boss at the University of Birmingham, has been in touch to say there is no need to rush back from Antigua. This is such good news. I like to do what I say I will do and the striving to push on and get to the end in time to meet the deadline to be back in work was becoming a strain. The removal of this added pressure is a massive boost. Thank you, Zena!

Again southwesterly winds have prevailed and we were only able to make slow progress, as little as one nautical mile an hour at best, often it is only 0.5 knots. Some bigger banks of cloud have passed over us from the north, so the sun has not been so hot in the afternoon.

I phoned my sister Gill at 8.15pm to wish her a happy birthday. It was early morning on Friday in New Zealand so she had not yet gone out to work. She and her family are off camping this weekend to celebrate her birthday, relaxing at a lovely lake area in a pine forest - it sounds great! Just after the call to Gill, at 8.45pm we had to go on para-anchor again as we were starting to be blown backwards. The retrieval line went under the boat during the deployment, but James sorted it to prevent any tangles. Another wonderful sunset to close the day. I had a hair wash and ended up with comedy sticking out hair - time for another DIY haircut!

We checked the wind direction every few hours, some movement from west to south-west, but it was still from the west in the morning.

Position at 9pm: 18°29'N, 42°52'W

26th February 2010

Beech Boys' Blog

If you are playing 'Spot the Difference' you may have noticed we went backwards overnight! At 8.30pm our forward progress, although slow, became non-existent and we had no choice but to set up the para-anchor. We had been expecting the westerly winds, but managed to tiptoe along without the westerly winds noticing us for most of yesterday. Unfortunately we were eventually 'spotted' and the westerly wind strength became too much for us. So we both got some extra sleep overnight, but even on para-anchor we have drifted backwards and will have to row again some of the miles we thought we had ticked off our 'to do' list! The forecast suggests the winds will return to the east, but will also continue variable, so localised variations on wind direction are still possible. Hopefully we may be rowing again by the end of the day?

We continue to receive visits from the Storm Petrel, who likes to fly circuits round the boat for a few minutes before gliding away, skimming over the water's surface to one side of the boat or the other. The mastery of its flight is shown by its ability to almost stall over the water, put its feet on the surface in a 'walking' action and pick up something with its beak before flying on. Fascinating to watch! We have also been entertained by some synchronised aerial acrobatics. We think these birds are Fulmars with dark grey wing tops and back, white under wing and belly. A pair of them perfectly co-ordinated their gliding flight, weaving a convoluted path over the waves. Their flight is very graceful and totally effortless. Almost like our rowing!

The extra effort put into rowing yesterday has aggravated my left hand. The middle and ring fingers are quite sore and difficult to either straighten properly or to make a fist with. This began earlier in the row, but had been less of a problem until last night when it was very tender. Hopefully the enforced rest today will help.

We are still looking for the remote control. If we find it we will certainly try out the fast forward button!

<u>Ship's Log</u>

8.30am wind 270 degrees due west, so still no go. We checked the para-anchor lines, everything was fine. By 12 noon we had drifted back to 18°29'N, 42°45'W. It was hot, there was little cloud and so we tried to rest in the cabin. We went through the playlist on James' iPod and put together a new two hour mega mix to listen to when we return to rowing at night. We kept checking the wind, still 270 degrees at 9pm. We had our evening meal at sunset before turning in to get some sleep. Throughout the night we kept checking the wind direction. 300 degrees at 2am, 0 degrees at 6.30am.

27th and 28th February 2010

Beech Boys' Blog

We made it away from the para-anchor at 7.30am on the 27th. Overnight we had continued to check the wind direction and it eventually came round to the north, so we were well placed to make progress south. On para-anchor we had travelled south a few miles, but also east 10 miles. It felt cruel that the massive rowing efforts to steal those miles from the ocean on Thursday were then snatched away over the last 39 hours, but without the para-anchor we would have drifted considerably further and lost even more ground.

We have been on para-anchor long enough on this voyage to almost have enough material to write a book on '1001 Things To Do While On Para-anchor'. Our best game from the recent stoppage was 'Name That Tune'. One person 'played' the tune on the kazoo and the other had to guess what it was. Tunes successfully guessed included the theme to 'Star Wars', 'Stuck In The Middle With You', 'Tragedy' and 'Scooby Doo'. Despite four versions of it on the iPod, 'California Dreaming' couldn't be deciphered, while 'Popeye the Sailor Man' also proved to be illusive! A lot depends on whether the kazoo player can keep going without getting the giggles and thereby introducing a series of bum notes into the tune!

While on his rowing shift James watched a large fish jump out of the water at regular intervals. It managed to make five consecutive jumps. Suddenly a very large bird swooped down onto the water just ahead of the fish and proceeded to fly off with a small fish in its beak! We think the big fish had been chasing the little fish, so it would have been more than surprised to see its prey disappear before its eyes! We think the bird was a Frigate bird. It had black plumage and a forked tail. It seemed to like to circle and glide around most of the time, keen to spy another tasty meal from a lofty vantage point.

Last night, as we began our nocturnal rowing we were treated to a fantastic moonrise. Although it was not quite a full moon, once above the horizon the moonlight lay, stretched across the ocean like a gleaming silvery corridor. This magical corridor of light ended directly on the stern of 'Beech Boys', beautifully illuminating the path we had just rowed. Although 'Moon River' wasn't playing on the iPod, it was a classic moment, making the words from the song 'two drifters' and 'after the same rainbows end' seem very appropriate!

James had another wildlife moment during his night rowing with three dolphins swimming alongside for a good 20 minutes. When you are out there on your own at the oars, friendly dolphin company is very welcome!

Ship's Log - 27th February

We came off para-anchor at 7.30am.

Position at 7.30am: 18°26'N, 42°42'W.

The sea state was almost calm, the wind direction was northerly light. We decided to row southwest. It was good to be on the move again. Johan's forecast sounds as though more northeasterly and easterly winds are due. This will be a real bonus and will help to move us on.

I spoke to Christine on satellite phone, she will take the train to Euston tomorrow and meet up with Caroline in London. They will then fly together from Gatwick on 1st March to Antigua. Overall we have made some good progress reclaiming old ground, but have also travelled further south. Johan thinks we could finish on Day 82. James and I cleaned the boat hull and had a wash. My left hand is starting to feel better. Anti-inflammatory tablets are helping.

28th February 2010

Sunday 28th - we are starting to see the '1,000 nautical miles to go' mark look fairly close now. All being well we should pass this during Monday 1st March. It has been a long haul completing these last few hundred miles. As much a mental as a physical test, but with a good forecast for the coming week we are optimistic that we can close in on the 50 degree west longitude mark.

An extra boost this morning was finding a bag of dried apricots in today's rations, plus one of our favourite meals, beef and potato casserole. These surprises give a real lift, especially when the apricots taste so good. Tangy and juicy describe the tasting experience, along with thoughts of eating fresh apricots when back home in the Lake District! I have appreciated the advice of those who have offered advice on how to ease the pain in my left hand, also for those praying about it too. It has felt easier today, which is good news!

Ship's Log - 28th February

9am, spits of rain at breakfast, then sunny - some large banks of cloud from time to time. Following waves and wind has helped us to keep our boat speed at 2 knots, so four nautical miles covered each shift. An 'albatros' looking bird flew ahead, landed on the sea and watched us as we rowed past before flying on in front of us and repeating his observation of our rowing! James saw a 10 foot fish, light blue tail, dorsal fin, maybe a marlin? We made progress down to 18°4"N, now rowing due west to get to 50 degrees west. It feels so energising to be making some steady progress. Woodvale have given a forecast of 20 knots east-northeast and south-east winds for next week.

1st March 2010

Beech Boys' Blog

Can you succeed at the two litre bathing challenge? Although our water supply is limited, we do wash! However, water is rationed for this activity - no power shower here! The challenge is to wash your hair and your body without using more than two litres of water. We allow a container of water to warm in the sun, so you can use hot water for the challenge. Then using a clean bucket and sponge, away you go! Probably best done in the bath though! If you can manage it with some water left over, then you obviously have huge potential as an ocean rower and should go into further training immediately!

There is clearly a danger here of re-running a famous Monty Python sketch. "What? 2 litres! You were lucky! We only used to get 1 litre of water and we had to wash ourselves and clean all the house windows with it!" "That is nothing! We used to dream of getting 1 litre!"

More seriously it is worth reflecting on the fact that one in eight people in the world do not have access to clean water and sanitation. So when you turn on the tap to get your two litres of water you are already well ahead in the day compared to many other people. WaterAid, the charity we are supporting from the row, work to provide long-term sustainable solutions which enable communities to gain access to clean water and sanitation. Their website provides details of this important work.

Today we should pass through the '1,000 miles to go' barrier. So we will be looking at three digit numbers on our 'miles to go' countdown from here on in! We seemed to have dropped out of any helpful current for the moment, so it will be later than expected when we reach 999. We anticipate it will be 10pm. We have a packet of Jammie Dodgers lined up ready for the big celebrations on-board 'Beech Boys!' If you want to join in with a wider celebration then give us a cheer at 10pm, raise a mug of hot chocolate to us, or see if you can eat a packet of Jammie Dodgers quicker than us!

Ship's Log

There was a full moon last night, the clouds looked amazing, with only a few stars out. We could see very easily with bright moonlight. We took a photo of the moon setting as the sun rose. It is probably the last full moon before we arrive in Antigua - we do hope so! In the afternoon James rowed us into the current again - hurray! Boat speed was pleasingly around 2 knots. Christine and Caroline arrived in Antigua at 8.40pm, so we thought of them both around that time. We prayed for them today that they would have a great holiday, no illness, lots of energy, safe travel and peaceful hearts. It would be wonderful to arrive in Antigua before Caroline has to leave. We will need to keep on top of our rowing and daily routine to push the miles along, praying for favourable weather to help us. At 9.25pm on Day 56 at sea we now only have 999.5 miles to go to Antigua!

Position at 9.25pm: 18°N 44°17'W.

Moonrise at 10.10pm - fantastic!

2nd March 2010

Beech Boys' Blog

Joe the Swimmer - 1,000 miles to go

It may not have been as dramatic as breaking the sound barrier, but breaking the '1,000 miles to go' barrier was nonetheless a noisy affair on-board 'Beech Boys'. We had a few rousing cheers followed by a kazoo recital - favourite tunes included the 'William Tell Overture', 'The Dambusters March', 'Star Wars Theme', The Jungle Book's King of the Swingers ('I Wanna Be Like You') and 'When the Saints Go Marching In'! It was a very eclectic mix of music that brilliantly captured the moment and the spirit of the occasion. We then devoured a whole packet of Jammie Dodgers. The biscuits had been careful positioned in the evening sun, so the jam was soft and stretchy - a gourmet delight! If you joined in the celebration, we hope you had as much fun as we did. Maybe take time to order some more Jammie Dodgers for when we pass the '500 nautical miles to go' mark, or buy a kazoo?!

In many ways this felt better than when we passed the halfway point. Obviously we are now closer to our goal of reaching Antigua, but perhaps it was the combination of passing the 1,000 mile post and seeing the next target for our voyage, the 50 degree west mark, coming ever nearer that did it. Anyway we now have a clear focus and our next goal is to reach this. It isn't so far away - only 300 miles! The forecast for the remainder of the week is positive, so we will push on, aiming to achieve this by the end of the weekend.

As a distraction from rowing we watched a number of the 'albatros' type birds gather together to form a small group gliding this way and that over the waves and passing nearby the boat on a parallel path. The most we had previously seen together had been two, now there were eight. As we watched to see what they were doing we could see groups of flying fish leaping from the sea and this was what these birds were after. Every so often we thought a bird had crash landed in its pursuit, but then realised this was the moment it had caught its prey. There were certainly some spectacular acrobatics going on. These birds can either eat a lot of fish or their success rate for catching them wasn't as good as we thought, as it lasted for well over half an hour! It was absolutely fascinating to observe this wildlife action from such close quarters.

Ship's Log

Good overnight row, but after covering 20 nautical miles, it was slow during the day. Wind has dropped and is more southeast, so pushing us to the north. We have to row across the wind which is slower going. However, we are moving towards Antigua rather than away from it! We both feel we need to get more momentum into the day to keep the miles ticking over; we have to keep our focus. No big wildlife moments, just four of the 'albatros' type birds back to chase fish. Alan and Glenda have sent messages through to us as Christine has been in transit to Antigua. It is ace getting the messages again! If we are to get inside the existing father and son crossing time of 78 days we need to cover more miles, so we need a boost from wind and waves.

3rd March 2010

Beech Boys' Blog

Steady rather than spectacular is probably the best way to describe progress since we passed the '1,000 miles to go' mark. Winds have tended to be light and rather fickle in direction which hasn't helped. Having dropped down to 18 degrees north we have had quite a bit of southwesterly wind which has gradually moved us north again, despite trying not to let it! We certainly feel we have paid a price for each mile gained during the hottest part of the day. Over these last few days there has been a very little breeze to assist in moving the boat, or to help cool you down. However, our trend is westward, with 265 nautical miles now left before we hit the 50 degree west mark. As we have maintained the same timetable for our rowing shifts throughout the row it is interesting to see how shifts which used to be the time for watching the sunrise and sunset each day are no longer so. This gradual change certainly adds a new dimension to our day, as well as reminding us we are further west than we once were!

It has been brilliant to hear that Joe the Swimmer has developed his own following among Coniston Crusaders and particularly from the Lazers Group. Alan, who leads the group, has been creating a weekly storyline about Joe for their Friday evening meeting. This has been filmed on video and then shown to the group. It has included some dramatic stunt work for Joe at times! Any water action has been set up using water in the bath. Other characters such as Bubbles and a dolphin called Dan have also been featured. We are looking forward to seeing the set of films when we return! They sound absolutely wonderful. Alan's careful film direction is sure to make these films contenders for an Oscar, although we are not sure what category they would fit into best.

We are very grateful that all our electrical systems are operating so well. It is reassuring to have the reliability this brings. It also helps keep the structure of our day, as things work as and when needed and time isn't used up on problem solving. It means a lot when you are busy with everything else not to have any additional issues to contend with.

We originally calculated the row was the equivalent of 600 lengths of Coniston Water. Best get back to completing the remaining 240!

Ship's Log

Speed overnight was down to 1.5 knots. At 9.30am during my rowing session there was a southeast wind, so we experienced slight crosswinds and odd wave pattern. By midday the wind speed increased and the wave pattern became more even. We began to average 2.5 knots and were covering around five nautical miles each two hour session - we were grateful for this!

Really good messages from Christine, who is now at the Beach Club in Antigua, she seems to be enjoying 'paradise'! We were pleased to hear of her travelling stories - people volunteering to carry luggage and help with taxis.

It has been encouraging to hear that Vicky McDougall is doing a WaterAid day at her school in Sheffield on Friday 5th March. Janet Vickers has also been in touch and her message spurs us on. Janet says James is a legend! We are both feeling good about covering the miles more speedily, although we need to be careful not to get pushed north. We have decided we need to use more treats, both to gain extra calories and to keep boosting our morale and because we have them! Over 20 flying fish suddenly came out of the water around tea time. 'Albatros' type birds tried to catch them but they all missed!

4th March 2010

Beech Boys' Blog

Hurray! Today should be our best 24 hour run to date - a following easterly wind and a sea that built through the night really assisted to push us on and helped get us through the 50 nautical miles in 24 hours mark. It is pleasing to have the speedier progress. Although bigger waves require more concentration when rowing, especially in the dark of night, they provide some welcome free energy. So no complaints about getting to Antigua more rapidly!

Today we thought we would provide some interesting facts about life on 'Beech Boys' so here we go:

A one metre square of the deck in front of the main cabin serves as the location for the following - the galley, laundry, bathroom, changing area to get into cabin, sitting area, sun cream application area, stretching exercise area and a second rowing position - although not all activities can happen at the same time!

We have three packs of cards with us, partly a result of the contents of the Christmas Crackers!

We have three books with us: a Pocket New Testament, Treasure Island and a Crossword Puzzle Book.

We get about six hours sleep a day, although not in one go, the longest sleep time is about 1 hour 45 minutes. We row in two hour shifts, but sleep time is lost getting in and out of the cabin, eating a snack and using the loo!

We have the James Bond books on iPod as audio books and are now on our second run through. We listen to these at night-time when rowing.

We drink between six and seven litres of fluid a day: made-up energy drinks, plain water and hot or cold chocolate.

The Antigua flag we have on-board (which we will hoist when we arrive) was acquired by bartering in the chandlery shop in La Gomera. We swapped half a reel of marine electrical cable for the flag and some rope!

We had an Arctic Tern fly over the boat this morning. It did some spectacular dives to catch fish, which was entertaining to watch.

<u>Ship's Log</u>

Great overnight run and by 1.30pm 54 miles were covered - this was our personal best to date. At 9.30am we had a fairly big sea, windy and very overcast. A lovely sunset was a superb bonus in an otherwise difficult day - we got a photo.

5th March 2010

Beech Boys' Blog

Well it's certainly a round of ups and downs this ocean rowing! Having been so positive about our good progress, overall yesterday proved to be a hard day. I had one session on the oars where I felt very weary and with the miles not clocking up so rapidly it felt even worse. When you are trying hard to push on and it is just not happening it feels uncomfortably tough! James came out of the cabin at 11am. As I rowed along it was good to be able to talk to him about how I was feeling. James passed me a mug of water which helped to freshen me up.

As there where larger waves yesterday and again today, the stern hatch to the cabin was kept closed because of the possibility of waves spilling in. As a result without the through flow of air the cabin was ridiculously hot. James decided to sleep with his head by the main hatch which was open as it was away from the waves, but he still got too hot and ended up feeling rough for a while. He took plenty of drinks in order to rehydrate and the fresh air out on deck gradually helped him feel better. It was a serious reminder that dehydration can quickly create problems. Our rest times have certainly become less comfortable, as we are forced to be outside in the sun. So between us we have both had our moments! We think the combination of not sleeping so well the previous night and just finding ourselves a little more fatigued in the heat have just taken their toll.

To cap it all, in the late evening when the waves had died down I was trying to get a quick nap before my first night shift and had the stern hatch slightly open to get some air through. Unfortunately a rogue wave caught the stern so we had a good splash of water illegally enter what should be our dry space on the boat! The quick dry towel over the mattress took the worst of it along with my head and shirt! Fortunately the laptop and satellite phone were packed away properly - so no damage was done! We managed a laugh afterwards, as I thought of the line from 'Shrek' where they approach the castle guarded by the dragon and donkey smells the brimstone, "I had my mouth open and everything!" It was a bit like that. I got a mouth full of seawater and everything! The waterproof mattress from Goacher Sails proved its worth and no real harm was done - just a further knock at the end of a difficult day. We could have done without it! However, laughter is a good medicine and we went into the night-time row determined to make a good job of it.

We are closing down on the 50°W mark, with 166 nautical miles to go so we should be there on Monday 7th. Our sights then move to the '500 miles to go' post.

Finally if you are getting in supplies of Jammie Dodgers for the '500 miles to go' celebration, it looks as though we may have to switch to Jelly Babies at this end, since our ship's biscuit ration is running low!

Ship's Log

The cargo ship 'Cala Palma' passed to the stern of us, going south at 5.30am. The ship was extremely well lit, especially the crew accommodation at the stern of the vessel. So it was easy to judge our position relative to their course and be happy we would miss each other! We are both getting weary as sleep has not been possible in the afternoons or early evenings. Southeasterly winds have meant we have rowed slightly across the wave pattern, but have covered about 45 miles, not bad considering...

6th and 7th March 2010

Beech Boys' Blog

Our progress west continues, the winds are southeast now, so we are rowing almost across them to get close to the course we want and avoid being pushed north. A nice north-east or easterly breeze would suit us well at this point! To add to the problems of the day, on Friday afternoon James tweaked a muscle in his back. It was too hot to be in the cabin and he was sitting on the second rowing position during his rest time when he suddenly felt something give in his back. There is no back support and with the side to side rolling movement of the boat he strained something in his mid-back just below the shoulder blades. It is proving to be really sore and making movement around the boat difficult and rowing extremely painful. For the time being we have rearranged the rowing shifts. I rowed longer shifts so that James could lie down in the evening and give his back some recovery time. James felt today was his worst day since feeling ill earlier in the voyage. Things will hopefully pick up again tomorrow. Above our cabin door we have the verse from Philippians, 'I can do everything through Him who gives me strength.' A positive thought to hold on to.

To help James I massaged his back before and after each rowing shift. He was able to do some 'careful' rowing so we at least covered some miles and I could still get a break. James had some extra rest on Saturday and Sunday mornings. Hopefully his back will continue to improve, otherwise there is more rowing for me!

A number of people have kindly emailed to ask how my hand is doing. This started to become a problem several weeks ago with painful knuckle joints on the left hand. Several people have suggested practical things to help ease it, also a number of people have told us they are praying for it to improve. Note to Richard in Birmingham and Lydia's group in Sheffield, it is improving and not as sore as a week ago when it was an effort to start rowing. Now it only takes a few strokes for my hand and me to get over the shock!

Ship's Log - 6th March

We were both feeling tired and had to work at getting motivated for the day. Southeasterly winds again, but they became lighter as the day went on. We are trying to get south, but the south-easterly wind continues to hold us north of 18 degrees north. At least we're able to travel west, but not getting very much help from the waves and wind. James is going carefully, rowing shorter sessions and taking ibuprofen for his back. I have aimed to row a few longer shifts so James can rest more. In the evening James is doing better, but side waves move the boat in an awkward fashion and make his back more uncomfortable. I have started to read out loud the classic story 'Treasure Island' and have carried it on again today. This 'Jackanory' time is helping James take his mind off his sore back. A good distraction tactic!

We were excited to find some extra food supplies today, which had accumulated from uneaten meals earlier in the row. We found chocolate in the unopened food bags and are treating ourselves to these bars over the next few night shifts. We have taken some time out to discuss and pray about keeping our focus and motivation to get the job done. During the mid-afternoon we saw jet vapour trails across the sky. They made us think of our flight home, and we wondered where that aeroplane was going.

Position at 8.45pm: 18°13.5'N, 48°8.9'W

Ship's Log - 7th March

The mid-Atlantic 5.30am rush hour. In the early morning, the AIS sounded, James woke from his sleep in the cabin and let me know there was a ship on a parallel course to us. We were travelling west, the other vessel east. It was a comfortable passing distance of two nautical miles. As I rowed along I watched the navigation lights disappear over the horizon. Then surprisingly the AIS started bleeping again. This time indicating a vessel that would pass to the stern of us. The glow of ships lights became apparent and as I rowed along I had a good view of it. It wasn't dangerous, but a curious and reasonably close passing of ships in the night! We could only be amazed that with so much water to work with, three boats all passed so close to one another within a 45 minute period. If we do this journey again we'll need to remember to leave more time in order to miss the traffic at this point!

We are both feeling tired from the further reduction in the amount of sleep we get. We were usually able to snatch some zzz's in the afternoon, but the cabin is as hot as a sauna in the afternoon with no stern hatch open. It is not a happy place to get forty winks! We hope to return to a situation where we can use the cabin to sleep in during the afternoons shortly. Overnight the wind has been from the south and continues from this direction today, resulting in more rowing 'across the grain.' Not much speed for us and with James' sore back it is very uncomfortable for him. We are both feeling a bit low from the demands of the last few days and digging deep, taking encouragement from the messages sent via the race website. The verses from Joshua, 'Be strong and courageous, for the Lord your God is with you wherever you go' are particularly helpful bringing inner strength. We are very much taking a day at a time.

There were southerly winds overnight and throughout the day, so slow progress was made as we rowed across the wind again. James' back is still not good. To help him manage the discomfort of his back I have been continuing to give him massages. Firstly just to ease his back so he can get outside the cabin and then again when he gets to the rowing seat before he starts rowing. Moving about a lively boat is difficult anyway and even more so when those movements are causing pain. Today we decided to make use of some stronger pain relief, diclofenac - James is now on two 50mg tablets per day.

There is practically no cloud, so hot all day. Read out today's episode of 'Treasure Island', 5-6pm while James rowed. He said it helps take his mind off his back. Anyway if you are into your soaps, forget the Rovers Return and The Queen Vic. It's all happening at the Admiral Benbow Inn! "Aha, Jim lad!"

James tried to access the MailASail weather forecast download, as we are unsure about the best way to proceed with the current weather. We are aiming to get further south, mainly to benefit from more favourable winds. At the moment the wind is obviously against us! Every time we get close to 18 degrees north, the winds have pushed us back to the north.

Position at 9pm: 18°14.9'N, 48°34.4'W

8th March 2010

Beech Boys' Blog

Opening food bag

We are closing down on the 50 degree west mark, with just 68 nautical miles to go, we should be there on Tuesday 9th. Our sights then move to the '500 miles to go' post!

We had hoped for better progress over the weekend, however southerly winds have meant we have been rowing across the waves in order to head west. We have had to persevere with this approach, as we do not want to get pushed further north. Hopefully some east or northeast wind will enable us to get below 18 degrees north. We have been trying to do this for the last week or so, only to then get south or south-east winds hindering any further progress in that direction.

James is still troubled with back pain. He has had some extra rest lying in the cabin, but when it's hot that just doesn't work. By re-arranging our rowing patterns James is still able to row. This is a massive effort on his part. Watching him struggle to get into salopettes to row at night is not easy. We are working flexibly on how long any of his shifts are, conscious that too much exertion could mean James is unable to row at all. When he feels able James is still rowing a full two hours, but at a gentle pace. It's tough going. If we had a following sea, the movement of the boat would be quite different and would make life much easier. The sideways rolling of 'Beech Boys' only serves to irritate his back and apply more pain.

Ship's Log

James spotted the big fish at 9am that had made an appearance last week. It is an impressive 12 feet or so with a blue fin.

James' back is showing some signs of getting better. We have been given some advice on stretches he can do. The painkillers will also be having an effect as he has taken these for several days now. Strong southeasterly winds - 15 knots became south during the afternoon - it is really frustrating rowing with these side waves and we don't manage to cover much ground. We spoke to Christine via her Skype telephone number, but couldn't hear her very well which was disappointing (especially since she could hear us clearly). We decided not to bother with it again, which is a pity as this would have been a cheaper phone call. The weather forecast indicated easterly and east northeasterly winds for tomorrow, so we will try and get down to 17 degrees north. It is interesting to see our current position is bang on the original track we marked on the chart as our intended route, so good navigation so far. We are all too aware of how much the wind can influence our progress - we would certainly appreciate some good winds to help us from now on.

9th March 2010

Beech Boys' Blog

Norman in the office

From early afternoon yesterday until well into the evening we had southerly winds which made rowing west the best we could do, with no chance of really getting south. Some of the wave patterns were awkward to negotiate as they were coming at us from different directions! Large side waves can also make the oarsman appear to be doing some sort of 'body popping' dance! As a wave lifts the oar the hand holding it is lifted, that side of the boat is then lifted - tending to make the rower lean over away from that side of the boat. The boat then drops down the back face of the wave and produces a lean from the rower in the opposite direction, this time followed by a lifting of the other oar hand! If you imagine Thunderbirds puppets, it may help to picture the peculiar nature of this movement. The rower isn't trying to do this on purpose, as it is not a normal rowing action. It is the comedy movement the ocean waves impose upon us. It would be quite funny to watch, but when you are trying to keep the boat moving, the disturbance to the rowing rhythm only serves as an annoyance! The southerly wind has contributed to our slowed progress, which is frustrating and it will be at least another day to get past 50 degrees west on our current form.

James' back continues to be painful. Parts of each day see some improvement, but it is not easy for him. I continue to provide a physio service before and after each of James' rowing shifts. Thank you to real physiotherapist Pauline (Christine's sister) for her advice. It is fortunate that James took out the Ocean Physio Cover policy before we started! He has Home Start and Work Station cover, so can be 'treated' in his home (the cabin) or at his work place (the rowing seat). It's a pity he didn't pay the extra for the Recovery option. The policy states, 'If the rower is unable to be economically repaired on the water, the policy holder with up to three passengers can be rowed to the nearest port.' Now that could have been handy!

Currently we have a southeasterly wind, but closer to south than east. This has been the pattern during the last few days, with the wind increasing in strength and changing to be southerly in the afternoon. It would be very encouraging for us not to see this happen again! At this point we still have 715 miles to cover to get into English Harbour in Antigua. It all seemed to be getting closer when we were covering 40 miles plus a day! We are optimistic that progress will improve again and just have to keep our minds on the task for each day.

Ship's Log

Another day with south-easterly winds becoming southerly. We have managed to keep on track, heading west without drifting north, but it is all very slow. Janet Vickers has emailed us with back exercises for James, which are very helpful. It was very kind of her to give us some good advice. No new weather updates, but we trust that tomorrow we can make a southwest course down to latitude 17 degrees north. At 11am we watched two Frigate birds frantically flapping their wings as they manoeuvred just above the water. They were 50 metres behind us and were trying to catch a small fish that a bigger fish was chasing! It was spectacular to watch, but we are not sure if they caught the fish! At 6.30pm dolphins splashed out of the water and jumped five or six times together in quick succession, sometimes clean out of the water, although not always close to the boat. For 20 minutes they provided us with some spectacularly acrobatic evening entertainment.

10th March 2010

Beech Boys' Blog

The story is pretty much the same. Southeasterly winds became southerly late morning. At least yesterday the waves were more in a pattern, so that helped us in our journey across them. When they are close together the boat feels as if a giant hand is just rocking it from side to side, as we bob up and down the waves. We now have a new term on-board - the slam dunk! If a wave breaks onto the side of the boat it sends up a vertical splash of water that then drenches the rower as it lands on them - you certainly know when you have been slam dunked!

Today we had a lighter southeast wind so we tried to row a more southwesterly course, however from midday that became harder to do and we knew we would do well to just keep a westerly course. Having revised our arrival day at 50 degrees west on several occasions it now looked as though this was the day for it! Overnight we went through the '700 miles to go' mark. We didn't have enough speed up to smash through it, but nonetheless that milestone has now passed! At 12.45pm we had 695 nautical miles to go.

The afternoon distraction of the next instalment of 'Treasure Island' continues and we both enjoy this point in the day. James' back is seeing some improvement - thanks to Pauline and Janet for your advice.

The big fish was with us again this morning making some big swirls in the water. So far it is only James that has seen it properly and it is therefore known as James' fish! I have seen it make splashes on the surface, although it has remained hidden from my view. Having seen it make some splashes in the water this morning near to the bow of the boat, we both felt 'Beech Boys' being bumped by the fish as it then swam underneath us. However, it is a bit like the Loch Ness Monster - we need a photo to prove it is out there! Mind you, our digital camera is proving to be tricky for wildlife photography. The delay between pressing the button and the photo being taken means that quite often when you view the photo afterwards it is just ocean, rather than a dolphin, a whale or a bird! It will be difficult to get a picture to prove it is there, unless James captures it on the underwater camera - could be exciting to see!

<u>Ship's Log</u>

A bird that looked very similar to a Gannet flew around us for a while, 9.45 to 10am. James' back felt better until the early evening. We washed some clothes today and I had a hair wash in the evening. I spoke to Christine on the phone and was pleased to hear that she and Caroline are having a lovely holiday. It was motivating to listen to Christine describe how beautiful the island is - we want to join them ASAP! Johan's latest weather news showed more southeasterly and south-southeasterly winds, but some northeasterly to easterly winds after Saturday 13th, which could give us a good run into Antigua.

Position at 8.45pm: 18°04'N, 49°46'W

11th March 2010

Beech Boys' Blog

If you have already checked our position from the race website it is clear we have moved on somewhat from the last few days. We can now report our 'escape' from the guardians of the 40 degree longitude! This has been quite a 'hush hush' operation which we have been planning for the last few days. While reading 'Treasure Island' we have used our black belt origami skills to produce a replica of 'Beech Boys' which we have had to keep folded in sections in the cabin until the right moment. Taking advantage of the complete calm of last night and with no moon in the sky, just a mass of stars, we let the replica become a decoy craft as we sped away at an impressive 1 knot! OK, the decoy boat is a made-up bit of the story! However, the calm conditions did begin our exit from the 40 degree longitude zone.

Overnight the absence of a breeze enabled us to easily head southwest and at the 5.30am change of rowers, James was able to report we had a slight following breeze. After a 10 minute tactical conversation on the best course to go, west or southwest, we continued southwest and James went into the cabin to sleep. A large cloud began to smother the stars and the wind was rapidly strengthening and within a few moments a lively squall was propelling us along at a fair 2 to 3 knots. The strong wind brought with it some heavy pulses of rain. As I rowed along I could smell a surprising flowery fragrance! This was followed by a stinging sensation in my left eye. Then I remembered that I had washed my hair earlier that evening, but must not have rinsed all the soap out! For a moment I thought we had turned into a drive-through car wash!

The wind dropped a little, but remained very steady. So just before 12.00 noon today we left behind the 40 degree longitude zone and rather like a cork popping out of a champagne bottle, entered the 50 degree zone. By heading southwest we have also managed to get below 18 degrees of latitude.

So after far too many sluggish and frustrating days we are grateful for the sudden and rapid change in our circumstances. It didn't fit with any weather forecast we had, but that doesn't matter! Thanks to everyone willing on and praying for the winds to change. Also anyone who has been blowing in the direction of Antigua! There are forecasted easterly winds over the weekend, hopefully these will arrive and enable us to progress with a speedy run through to the finish.

James continues to take the tablets and carry out the physio advice to ease his back. All being well the following waves will be more comfortable for his back when rowing than the side waves we previously had. This morning he felt it was better, although possibly the adrenalin of some exciting night -time rowing may have served to override the normal discomfort he has had! However, signs of improvement are there for which we are thankful.

Our next goal is clearly the '500 miles to go' mark. It is getting closer, with only 170 miles to cover until we reach that point. It will be a big moment and we will celebrate it in style as we break open a bag of Jelly Babies!

<u>Ship's Log</u>

We think the squall that got us going southwest during the night may have been fairly localised. We thank God for answering our prayers for a more helpful wind direction - God will make a way. We rearranged the food stores for days 81 to 90 which were in the front cabin, relocating them to the deck lockers.

There is a good feeling aboard 'Beech Boys'. It is so encouraging to be able to move more positively and gain ground to Antigua. We received a terrific email from Asker Jeukendrup from the School of Sport and Exercise Science at the University of Birmingham. It gave us a fantastic boost as we read it. Here it is .....

"Hi Guys,

Superb stuff! I am in admiration of the achievements! Every day I read your exploits with great interest!

I have worked with several expeditions, extreme events, world class athletes and I think I can therefore say that I have a fair amount of experience. However, I don't think I have ever seen a crew that kept the spirits so high for so long! Fantastic stuff! Maybe it is the father-son thing but whatever it is, it is pretty unique and something to be proud of!

All the best, all the strength in the world!

Keep those spirits high!   Asker"

12th March 2010

<u>Beech Boys' Blog</u>

Variety is the spice of life! After some impressive displays of night-time stars of late, last night was totally overcast and the calm conditions from the early evening continued well into the night. This made for quite an odd feeling as you rowed along enveloped in darkness, with the boat resting fairly flat upon the water. The only contrast to the dark that surrounded us was the outline of the boat lit by the navigation light. During our rowing sessions last night we both heard the sound of passing aircraft. Although not visible, the engine noise is quite impressive. We wondered where they are heading. We must be getting closer to civilisation!

Breakfast was different today because it was raining. This was our first experience of daytime rain. It had been wet before dawn and continued through to midday. As a bonus, it brought with it a following breeze which helped our progress. In fact the rain was quite refreshing, as the air temperature was high, but after a couple of hours of rowing your hands look rather wrinkled from being so wet! The daytime sky was also different. No blue with a few white clouds. Instead, lots of contrasting greys and the suggestion every so often of a break in the expanse of grey and that perhaps this was the last rain cloud heading our way! It didn't brighten up until the afternoon, however the rain certainly washed the salt from the boat. While seawater is obviously salty, mid-ocean it is particularly so. Splashes of water onto the boat leave impressive salt residues when dry.

Approaching rain cloud

We had to monitor power use carefully today. The solar panels do recharge in cloudy conditions, but obviously not as quickly. Our watermaker is the single biggest power user on 'Beech Boys', so that was on for a shorter spell today. We carried forward a small reserve of water from the previous day to provide for such eventualities.

We experimented with a different grip on the oar handle. Christine had made up some tubes of sheep's fleece to go over the foot straps, so they wouldn't rub if we rowed bare foot. As we have been rowing in trainers these haven't been used. The fleece tubes fit exactly over the oar handles and have proved to be very comfortable, although they do look a little odd. All we need now are some furry dice!

Hopefully by Monday or Tuesday we should reach the '500 miles to go' mark. It would be brilliant to arrive at a huge neon lit sign in the ocean that said 'Antigua 500 miles!' As this isn't likely we will have to take the word of our GPS system that we have reached that point.

Ship's Log

Overnight it was very overcast and I discovered that I needed some different glasses! The rowing position is just too far from the GPS repeater for me to be able to read it in the dark and rainy conditions. By keeping the hand bearing compass on the deck in front of me if I wear my reading glasses I am able to check the course as I row along. It does mean I have to row with my head bent forward to look at the deck which alters my rowing stroke, but at least we are going in the right direction!

Following waves are moving us on more quickly. Most of the day has been wet, with some very heavy showers from the south. Visibility becomes very limited in torrential downpours. We managed to organise our lunch in the dry. James' back is manageable today. The overcast afternoon means we can get into the cabin for some sleep, as it is not so hot, and we both feel much better for it.

Again it means a lot to us to receive our email messages. As we make progress to Antigua with an easterly wind, it just feels as though it would be good to be there now! We're going to try a new three hour rowing and resting rotation tonight if James' back allows him to row that long. I certainly feel in need of more sleep, as I am starting to feel tired more often. The rain has been refreshing, although quite a few pairs of soggy shorts, socks and waterproof jackets now need to be dried. It rained all day and most of the night right up to 6am. Superbly James was holding his own, managing to cope with two and a half hours of torrential rain on his night shift.

13th and 14th March 2010

<u>Beech Boys' Blog</u>

Sunshine after the rain sums up Saturday morning. Following some heavy spells of rain through Friday afternoon and overnight we can start to dry out! All our experience of Lake District weather has paid off, as we had one spell of rain giving over an inch of rainwater as measured in our plastic beaker rain gauge in a 2.5 hour downpour.

Waking up in the cabin to the noise of heavy rain bombarding the hatch covers does not make the prospect of a return to the oars an attractive one! However, we both know the other person needs to get inside having been on the receiving end of the aerial deluge! By careful timing of our changeovers, i.e. rowing a bit longer until the rain eases off, has meant we have managed to keep the cabin dry. We have a big plastic bag to put wet gear in as we come into the cabin. We then put the wet stuff on when we go back on shift. James had the longest spell of heavy rain to deal with overnight and we both had a laugh when it came to the changeover. I picked up my trainers which were outside the cabin door only to find they were completely full of water! Our Gill foul weather gear has been first rate and fully tested these past few days! Waterproofs on, the smell of Campingaz, the sound of the stove going, eating hot food with your back turned to the wind and rain to prevent the packet of hot food becoming full of rainwater! James thought the day reminded him of camping expeditions he had been on! Our preparations in Coniston have certainly helped when it comes to dealing with rain.

Saturday and Sunday night - now that James' back has enabled him to row for longer we have started a three hour night-time rowing shift. The longer shifts are to help us gain some better quality sleep. It also means we lose less valuable sleeping time, as there are fewer changeovers! It has worked well and we don't wake up feeling as groggy as we had done before. Glen at University of Birmingham Sport was reading the blog of Annie and Mel from 'Team Explore' and spotted they had successfully done this and passed the idea on. We think it will take a few days to properly establish our new system, but already we are experiencing some benefit.

Beautiful sunrise and then clear skies for most of the day - back to hot! We rowed together for an hour, between 11 and 12 noon, which was good fun! Last night's experiment of three hour shifts to provide extra sleep is a winner. I certainly found it enabled me to catch up with myself again! Fatigue makes everything harder to deal with, so in this final stage of the row it is worth keeping as fresh as we can. The overnight easterly has turned to the southeast, but while gentle, has still helped us along. We are trying to keep the momentum of the boat going well, currently 2 knots. Hurray! James' back is improving, he just needs to avoid overdoing it. James' hair wash this evening has refreshed him. I called my mum but had to leave a message on the answer machine.

Position at 8.55pm: 17°46.9'N, 51°29.9'W

It was interesting to see that the crescent moon had just risen and was visible for a few minutes before the sunrise. The sunrise was very close to the point the moon had appeared above the horizon. It is another scorching day here, with the wind from the southeast now that the sun is up. Overnight it had been getting very close to southerly which was making progress slower for us. A good run of easterly or northeasterly winds would be just the ticket for us now to see us home. We keep giving ourselves a daily target to work at, as we aim to row down these final miles.

We did remember it was Mother's Day! Satellite phone did the job enabling us to speak to our mums, while flowers sent from Bunches also helped pass on the messages of love and appreciation to our mums - they are brilliant!

Ship's Log - 14th March

I found the 8.30-11.30am shift hard going today. The winds were from the south so a side-on wave pattern continually made it awkward to establish a smooth rhythm to my rowing. Inevitably this plays on your mind as the slower boat speed is plain to see on the navigation panel in front of you. The name of the game is to avoid being distracted by the mental dimension, the discouragement of not going so fast and not giving in to any feeling of despair that you are struggling to make the progress you wanted to. In the last two days we made 40 miles each day, so we are certainly doing better than we had been! There has been hot sunshine through the day, with just a little cloud in the early evening. We washed clothes today and I had a hair wash. James read out our email messages, which cheered us up. There were more Frigate bird antics to watch as they caught fish near to the boat. James rescheduled our night-time three hour shifts to be closer to the sleep times we had got used to already, which was a good idea. At 9pm, our GPS showed we only have 51 miles to row before we reach the '500 miles to go' mark. We can do it - we will do it - we *will* get there!

Position at 9.15pm: 17°44.6'N, 52°0.89'W

15th March 2010

Beech Boys' Blog

As we creep up on the '500 nautical miles to go' mark it looks as though it will be late tonight or Tuesday morning before we can celebrate. Today's weather has dealt us another southeast breeze card. The wind is strong enough to produce more of the awkward side waves again. Unfortunately it has already a lot of south to it and as the tendency has been for the wind to increase during the afternoon and move round to the south it once more signals that it could be slow hard work. However, when the moment arrives we are ready with Jelly Babies and our last cup of hot chocolate powder saved just for the occasion.

Frigate birds have stayed close to us over the last few days. They have a big wing span and gracefully, effortlessly, soar at height over the water to spy out fish. Once they have located their prey they swoop down quite rapidly to the water's surface. Then in marked contrast to their gliding skills they put great energy into a flapping 'dance' to enable them to hold station over the surface and quickly change direction as needed in order to catch a jumping fish. It is extraordinary to watch as well as good entertainment value.

We had a 'supermarket trolley sweep' through our food lockers to check on stock. It also provided the opportunity to re-arrange things as far as the boat trim was concerned. Overall we have been pleased with our on-board diet. There are a couple of meals we have not enjoyed so much, but the variety of food has been sufficient for it to never get boring. Although at this point in the row we would both like more biscuits and chocolate! These are now in short supply, and will be occasional treats for the remainder of the voyage. The late decision to bring tubes of condensed milk proved to be a culinary success story. It has been added to porridge, a biscuit dessert we make ourselves, custard and even on occasion taken on its own as comfort food! We would never use it at home!

The ship's doctor has had less work to do of late. Both patients have been improving and told to "Keep taking the tablets!" So if you need a doctor's appointment this week you shouldn't find the queue quite so long. James has been able to move more comfortably about the boat and get to the end of a rowing session without feeling so sore. My hand is less painful, although the middle and ring finger still don't straighten properly. Once rested after the row it should recover and be back to normal.

The three hour night-time row and sleep pattern is now well established and we will continue with this until we reach Antigua. Most significant has been the fact we have felt much fresher when waking. We had started to think that we were living our lives with some odd time zone operating on-board. Two hours of rowing felt like four! Yet only a few feet away in the cabin if you went to sleep for two hours it only felt like you had just closed your eyes two minutes ago! The alarm beeping away, telling you to get up again, had to be wrong!

Ship's Log

Overnight we had a southeasterly breeze. It was warm outside, there was no moon. The stars were out, with a small amount of cloud. At 9am good sized waves from the southeast gave a fair bit of rock and roll to the boat! I fell off the rowing seat during this session when a big wave hit the side of the boat! It didn't wash me off the seat, but the lurching of 'Beech Boys' in response to the wave was sufficient to remove me from my perch. I ended up sitting in the space between the gunnel and the seat rail with my feet still in the foot straps! Fortunately no injuries, just the difficulty of rearranging myself back onto the rowing seat!

After lunch the sea became quieter and the wind dropped in strength to become a gentle southeasterly in the evening. We made further progress south through the day. Some great messages passed onto us by Christine via email - people willing us on through the '500 nautical miles to go' mark. We should make that early on the 16th March between 6 and 7am. Again it was very hot with little daytime cloud cover. Today we also finished the reading of 'Treasure

Island'. We have really enjoyed the daily 'Jackanory' time, although trying to keep all the character accents going wasn't easy.

We're sticking with our new night-time rowing patterns - 7.30-10.30pm: James, 10.30-1.30am: Norman, 1.30-4.30am: James, 4.30-7.30am: Norman. After this, we row in two hour shifts through the day. We know now there is only a very slim chance of getting inside the existing father and son's record crossing time of 78 days. To do this we would need to average 65 miles a day, which so far we have not done, so that record seems to have slipped away from us.

16th March 2010

Beech Boys' Blog

This is Day 71 at sea. We finally reached the '500 nautical miles to go' mark at 11.28am - yippee!

Celebrations followed with a packet of Jelly Babies. Joe wanted to be in the photo of the GPS display which showed 499 to go and then fell off as a wave rocked the boat! Fortunately no harm done! It has been good to reach this point and we now feel significantly closer to the end of our voyage. We are aware our progress has been slower in recent days, so based on what we have managed to row of late we have set a daily goal of 35 miles to cover. Hopefully we can better this. If we meet our target we should be in English Harbour, Antigua, in 15 days, which sounds really good from where we are sitting.

James' back has been affected by the action of the side-on waves yesterday and it was pretty uncomfortable for him again overnight. We could do with these easterly winds turning up to give an easier motion to the boat. They would also get us to Antigua a little more speedily! So James is still having the massage treatment and is on pain relief to help make things tolerable. Thanks to everyone who has sent a message with advice on coping with this and expressing sympathy regarding his back.

Now for the news many of you have been waiting for. Completely undeterred after his fall from the GPS monitor, Joe finally plucked up courage to ask Bubbles to marry him! The excitement of crossing the '500 nautical miles to go' mark perhaps made it easier for him to ask, and for Bubbles to say yes! Further news will follow as wedding plans begin to come together over the coming week. So a double celebration today - marvellous!

Ship's Log

Since reaching the '500 nautical miles to go' mark the wind direction has not been helpful, turning from south-southeast, to south and then southwest. So during the afternoon and into the evening we have a headwind and we are being pushed north again. Gaining ground to the west is very slow, with a tough afternoon and evening of rowing. James' sore back is protesting at the conditions and we have a difficult decision as to whether to go onto para-anchor and try and have a period of rest, or push on and risk more problems for

James. The wind became lighter which prompted us to continue rowing. Easterly winds are due in on Thursday, but light south-southeasterly tomorrow, so this is hopefully what we get and it will keep us going.

It is too hot in the cabin - not easy to sleep, so that is another factor in not wanting to go onto the para-anchor. We will need to set up the boat for windier weather tomorrow. We used up the remains of our hot chocolate supplies and the last of the Jelly Babies with our evening meal as we celebrate passing under '500 nautical miles to go' - we raised our mugs and offered each other a congratulatory toast, "Cheers mate!" as we drank our hot chocolate. No Frigate birds today. The Storm Petrel was close by at one stage but it didn't stay for long.

Position at 9.15pm - 17°40'N, 53°11.8'W

Both a bit discouraged. Praying about other people rather than just ourselves helped us to re-focus. Joshua 1:9 'Be strong and very courageous'. Christine and Caroline saw Chris and Joe from 'HCL Workforce 1' finish today.

17th March 2010

Beech Boys' Blog

An unhappy return to a game we thought we had left behind 'Spot the Difference!' We have only progressed 15 miles since crossing the 500 mile mark. We should have turned on to the toll road and avoided all the hold-ups! It is disappointing to have set ourselves what we thought was a realistic and fairly modest target of 35 miles for each day to get ourselves home and then fall so short of it on the first day! Come on 'Beech Boys', get yourselves into Antigua!

It was quieter overnight and again this morning which should help us. The forecast is for strong east winds from tomorrow. These will certainly get us going and we will tick off some miles to the finish in a speedier fashion. Today we sorted some jobs on-board to get ready for windy conditions and bigger waves. If the forecast is right and we have four or five days of 20 knot plus winds it could be quite tiring. So having everything securely tied down, the boat trim set right and our food easily located will all help.

Just to mention Joe did have a 'ring' of sorts which he gave to Bubbles when he proposed. It was a heart shape silver pendant from one of the Christmas crackers! Not much in the way of jewellery shops out here, so it was going to be difficult for Joe to come up with anything that could be described as jaw -droppingly spectacular. The good news is Bubbles likes it and really that's all that counts!

Hopefully the green dot will move with more obvious progress during the rest of the week.

<u>Ship's Log</u>

This was a tricky day. James' back made rowing painful overnight and it was discouraging. After three hours of effort we made no progress against the headwind. We don't want to give in and have continued rowing throughout the day into the wind. At best 1.5 nautical miles rowed in an hour and a quarter. We cleaned the hull of barnacles and noticed the bows slightly too high in the water, so we have repositioned some kit to adjust this. I rowed through the afternoon and evening to give James some recovery time. James felt a bit better through the evening shift. He had taken a lesser dose of medicine as his back had improved, but we decided he just needs to keep on top of the medication with a full dose of pain relief so that he can row, otherwise we will be out here for a long time! James phoned his sister Lydia for a chat. How fantastic - she is able to come out to Antigua to see us in - wonderful! This has made our day and has spurred us on again. Up until that phone call this had been James' most difficult day of the voyage. Pain, discomfort and frustration at not being able to row properly in the conditions are a miserable mix. Suddenly this has been transformed with Lydia's news. Phone calls are a powerful medicine. Hopefully easterly winds for a few days now and we can make progress after two days of headwinds. James spotted a whale, but it didn't stay around for long.

Position at 9.30pm: 17°46'N, 53°24'W

18th March 2010

Beech Boys' Blog

Thanks to everyone who sent us a "Well done!" message for passing through to the last 500 miles of the row. We enjoyed reading them and hearing of the various Jelly Baby and hot chocolate moments you had as you celebrated with us!

It was good to have that encouragement, because while it was a lovely day on the ocean yesterday, much of the breeze was southwesterly and then in the afternoon westerly. This was torturously slow to row into and was too much for James' back. He has kept going with his stretching exercises, massages and a small amount of extra rest until the wind is more favourable, which have all helped. As the sun began to go down, the wind was very light and James tested his back again with some rowing which went well and he managed to row all his night shifts, although getting going for each one was a tough mission. We will just have to continue carefully with this each day in order to keep James operational! It would be preferable to feel the last few weeks at sea for both of us had been enjoyable, rather than a horror story!

We have used some time to put 'Beech Boys' through her 2,000 nautical mile service. So cleaning the hull, washing some clothes, repacking some of the food stores were all useful jobs taken care of. A few technical discussions were held yesterday regarding our equipment on-board 'Beech Boys'. This has enabled us to decide upon the winners of the 2010 'BBORAs' - Beech Boys Ocean Rowing Awards. The categories making up the awards were:

Most useful gadget - Gerber multi tool, sponsored to us by Cotswold. We have lost count of the number of times it has saved us getting the whole tool kit out. Just brilliant!

Most useful item we didn't mean to bring - an Irish linen tea towel with drawings of knots on it. Not actually used for drying up plates, but great for drying your hands on, wiping off water splashes and mopping up in general.

Best fun item - plastic kazoo!

Most mind boggling "How does it work?" item - the satellite phone and our ability to send and receive emails in mid-ocean.

Best motivational snack - Jammie Dodger biscuits.

The news many people have been waiting for - Joe and Bubbles have decided to go for a Caribbean wedding! They thought it was too good an opportunity to miss, so plans are being made, with some elaborate ideas being discussed. Whether *Hello!* magazine will wish to buy the photos is debatable, however it will be fascinating to discover their final plan and to obviously see the wedding itself!

We were thrilled to hear that Lydia will be in Antigua to see us finish! It had always seemed less than satisfactory that we would not be together as a family in Antigua. However, with our crossing being delayed, and taking longer than planned, her university exams are now over and she will be able to fly out and join Christine. We send a massive 'thank you' to Caroline Beckett for being out there in Antigua with Christine over the last fortnight. You have been a great support, assisting with the Antiguan arrangements for the finish. We are sorry you won't see us with Caroline, but we will visit and tell you all about it. You have been an absolute star!

<u>Ship's Log</u>

Overnight conditions became lighter, so rowing was easier, with southeasterly winds again for the last few hours before dawn. Some good meteors entertained us as they blazed across the night sky. A crescent moon appeared over the horizon at the point where the sun set - good to see it again! Through the day we had 5 knots of southeasterly and a short spell of southerly winds in the late afternoon before more east southeasterly wind in the evening. Five Frigate birds flew around us at the end of the day, finally heading off at sunset. One of them caught a fish which two other birds and a big fish had all been chasing after too!

James gave me a shoulder massage today, since my left shoulder has been feeling a little bit sore - maybe with too much rowing yesterday. His back is still troubling him and he is taking paracetamol between diclofenac doses. The massage and stretching routines continue. James has rowed his shifts, but in discomfort.

Christine sent messages through including part of 'Red Arrow's blog - it is good to hear other rowers' news and to hear about them nearing the finish. It also makes you wish you were there too! Although we find it a little discouraging knowing we have perhaps another 14 days at sea with our current boat speed. However this soon passes and James and I are looking forward to getting to Antigua ASAP and have set our thoughts to enjoy the remaining days of the voyage. The next four days forecast is 15 to 20 knots plus of east and north-easterly winds, so it could be demanding. We hope it stays below 15 knots, as we are tired and know we can manage that better. Philippians 4:6 'Have no anxiety about anything'. We tried porridge hot with sultanas and peanut butter as a pudding tonight - the verdict was a slightly surprising OK!

Position at 9pm: 17°44'N, 53°54'W

19th March 2010

Beech Boys' Blog

James at work

Seat belts are on and we are hanging on to our hats! The easterly wind arrived at the end of the evening and became stronger over night, so we are now moving westward a good deal faster. The waves are obviously helping too. We aim to time our oar strokes so that we are 'picked up' by the waves and surfed along them in order to save some of our energy. The wave pattern isn't particularly regular though and every now and then we have a large swell from the southeast - so there is plenty to concentrate on!

The GPS display shows we have 325 nautical miles to go in order to cross the 60 degree longitude mark. This is approximately the same distance we would drive to get from Coniston to Grandma Beech in Highcliffe, Dorset. In the car with stops it takes about eight hours, certainly longer by rowing boat, so a good job we don't normally row to Grandma's house! Once we reach 60 degrees of longitude the final part of the voyage is a mere 100 nautical miles into English Harbour. As the miles are ticked off we have to keep a closer focus on our position, as there is less and less sea room to play with if we are off course and we don't want to miss Antigua! Listening to other teams' reports of their approach it seems as though the winds haven't been doing what they normally do. So gauging the best final approach is going to be tricky. We plan to use the northeast wind forecast during some of the next few days to get us onto 17 degrees north. We will then have to look at the next five day forecast to see what to do regarding holding that position, or going further south.

It has been good to have news of other crews finishing ahead of us. We were all in La Gomera for so long that everyone got to know each other well. It is great to share in other people's success and the realisation of their own dreams to venture across the ocean. It also makes us want to be there! Unfortunately there is some further hard work for us to reach that end point. There are no shortcuts, or easy ways round it. We have to persevere, keep our focus on what we still have to do and keep smiling as we pull those oars through the water!

The encouraging comment in our food bag today was, 'Think about all those people who have helped get you this far'. It is amazing how many people have been involved in some way or other. We both know we would not be out here if that interest, help and support hadn't been there for us. We shout a loud "Thank You" to everyone who has helped us.

Safe travel home to Caroline and safe journey to Antigua to Lydia - our love to you both.

Ship's Log

Mileage covered has been creeping up over the last few days, from 31 to 40, and 52 today! Southeasterly, 15 knots of wind. This has pushed us north a bit, but hopefully we can get south again as the northeasterly arrives over the weekend. Spoke to Christine on the phone - she is trying to get some advice for us about the best approach into Antigua. James' back is coping, although he felt a bit sick this morning as the boat was moving around a lot in the waves, maybe just a bit dehydrated. After lying down and sleeping, he felt fine again.

Dolphins joined us briefly this afternoon. The boat trim seems good in the bigger seas. Overnight we wore our life jackets and as always we have leashes on when on deck during the day. We hope we can keep going next week as the strong wind and waves are forecast to continue - at least we can get there quicker! The cabin is VERY hot as we can't open the rear hatch with the big waves - we hope we can get enough rest. At 9.15am James saw a big fish jump a good 15 feet into the air as it powered out of a wave - truly spectacular! During the daytime we are covering about 5 nautical miles every two hours. It feels good to be closing in on Antigua.

Position at 9pm: 17°50'N, 54°46'W

20th and 21st March 2010

Beech Boys' Blog

It is wonderful to see the 'miles to go' figure getting smaller at a steady rate. However, the wind has been southeasterly since Friday afternoon through into Saturday, making it difficult for us to go south. In fact we have just managed to go west. Our concern is that if this continues for too long we will be too far above Antigua, with no favourable wind to help us line up for our approach. The forecast suggests easterlies - we hope they turn up soon. We can then work off this, moving south to 17 degrees north and then we would have a straight run in to Antigua. It certainly feels like we are playing the rowing boat equivalent of snakes and ladders! Not forgetting you have to throw the right number on the dice in order to finish!

Ship's Log - 20th March

Wind in the southeast, so we have to row across the waves to keep on course. It is frustrating to row in these conditions as the waves roll 'Beech Boys' and our rhythm goes. The forecast just in shows easterly then northeasterly winds of 15 to 20 and then 25 knots, so we will be flying along with these conditions - trust we will cope, particularly with 25 knots! Good food today - chicken tikka, beef and potato casserole, biscuits and Jelly Babies! James got a great photo of a Frigate bird.

It is very hot until the sun goes down - too hot in the cabin for me. We topped up the battery of the handheld VHF radio ready for Antigua. Christine has sent through information regarding other boats' positions when they crossed 60 degrees west. Most were on 17 degrees north and this will be our target. Overnight we travelled a bit to the north, but hope to regain some of this during the day.

Position at 9.20pm: 17°42'N, 55°28'W

One recent topic of conversation we have had over our evening meal was how you could improve the television programme 'Top Gear'? We think they should introduce a new feature called 'A Star in a Reasonably Priced Rowing Boat!' The celebrity would row around a course as fast as possible, but would also have to scrape barnacles off the bottom of the boat and eat a boil-in-the-bag meal without losing any of it while the boat rocked about! Perhaps Simon Chalk could be the RBS - Rowing Boat Stig?

<u>Ship's Log - 21st March</u>

We are both feeling positive and push on to reduce the miles. Lydia and her Sheffield cheerleading team have finished 3rd and 1st in different categories with their Air Hostess themed routine at Future Cheer, held in the Manchester Velodrome. She gets the train to London today and after a hotel stop will fly to Antigua tomorrow morning! We have rearranged our food stores, so they are all easy to get to tomorrow if the predicted 25 knots of wind turns up. We made extra water anticipating the cabin probably will not be usable in the daytime if the waves are big. The solar panels were able to recharge the batteries even while we ran the watermaker and the usual navigation equipment - impressive stuff.

We checked our chart calculations for a possible position that tomorrow's weather may push us to, which means more monitoring of our progress to check we don't go too far south. The forecast is for east and northeasterly winds. It has set our minds working on a possible arrival date. It looks as though it could be next Saturday, Sunday or Monday.

We had a pleasant surprise today when James found 60 euros in my Tilley hat - forgotten about from our time in La Gomera!

Position at 8.45pm: 17°33'N, 56°13'W

22nd March 2010

Beech Boys' Blog

Today is World Water Day! A year ago we launched 'Beech Boys' on Coniston Water to coincide with this. Now we are a few days from completing the row. We hope you take a moment to look at WaterAid's website www.wateraid.org/uk/ to find out more about their valuable work.

Besides the personal adventure and challenge of rowing across the Atlantic Ocean, we wanted to support something significant and we hope our efforts have drawn attention to the difficulties that so many people in poorer countries have to just access safe water and sanitation. Funds raised from the row will go to assist the work of WaterAid in Tanzania. We aim to help WaterAid change 2,000 people's lives through the provision of safe water and sanitation in their communities.

Once we had embarked on the project of rowing the Atlantic we became aware that the existing father and son record for the crossing was 78 days and felt that it could be challenged. However, to set a new record unfortunately became unrealistic some time ago. Too much time spent at the all inclusive para-anchor holiday resort and generally trying conditions out here on the ocean have hampered our progress!

However, we can still be the first British father and son to make the voyage. In some ways, perhaps that is better. Whatever time we set, will be beaten at some point. At least with being the first father and son from Britain to row across the Atlantic, you continue to be the first British father and son to achieve this! It is also good to acknowledge that James will be one of the youngest people to have rowed the Atlantic. He celebrated his 19th birthday during the row. He has certainly taken up the challenge of the event throughout. Basically when it is your turn to row there is nowhere to hide. You have to get out there and do it! He has acquitted himself well, with a truly superb and inspirational effort.

<u>Ship's Log</u>

Winds increased overnight to give Easterly 20 knots by 9am and 25 knots plus through the day. Cabin door was closed and the vent covers were on all day. Big waves, and an impressive following sea meant we covered 3.5 nautical miles in an hour. Top surf speed was 8.1 knots when James was driving! Difficult to decide on using the cabin at night with the door open on the latch as waves may still splash in, but the cabin will need air circulating if we are going to get some sleep. We were both pleased with miles covered today.

Position at 9pm: 17°15'N, 57°15'W

23rd March 2010

Beech Boys' Blog

Rather like Wallace and Gromit trying to take off in their rocket for the moon, it goes better with the handbrake off! Yes, we have to admit we have only just discovered the handbrake release button! Now it's off we are really moving. For some time we had looked at this button, but thought it was the ejector seat control and had therefore left it well alone!

Conditions yesterday afternoon were lively with 25 knots of easterly wind, so there were some large waves to contend with at times. Judging which waves not to surf is as important as trying to get some speed from as many waves as possible. Some of the waves do rear up to give a very steep face. When you are on the rowing seat you are literally looking up at the stern of the boat as it is lifted on the wave and looming above the cabin of 'Beech Boys' is the top of the wave itself! If you surf straight down a steep wave it can lead to the boat plunging its bow into the trough of the wave ahead. This acts as a very effective brake and as the stern of the boat is being pushed forward by the wave it is possible to 'pitch pole', with the boat going stern over bow - not recommended! So while going for speed we are taking care too.

We certainly had a number of waves spoiling the fun yesterday by 'slam dunking' us as we rowed along. It is a bit like the scene in Wallace and Gromit's 'The Wrong Trousers'. Where normally the jam fired by Wallace's breakfast machine hits a piece of toast popping up out of the toaster, Gromit has a moment where the toaster doesn't work and he gets covered in jam. You can see the wave about to hit the side of the boat, you are on the rowing seat, your feet in the foot straps and you can't move out of the way, but you know what is coming next! If only some giant piece of toast would pop up to act as a shield! Of course it doesn't and you are then left rowing completely soaked through. However, it is all about getting to Antigua and this is part of our ocean rowing experience - so we can't complain!

Overnight the easterly wind only eased a little, so today we covered over 75 nautical miles in 24 hours! This is our best day's run to date. It is not as windy today, but with it being an easterly we are going to be able to push through nicely to the 60 degree west mark. After this we have a final 100 nautical miles to cover to English Harbour. So with a continuation of these conditions it is looking as though we will arrive in Antigua over the weekend.

Joe the Swimmer and Bubbles' latest wedding news is that Joe's brother is going to be best man and a good number of Bubbles' relatives are coming across for the wedding ceremony in Antigua. They are hitching a ride in Lydia's luggage! In the end *Hello!* magazine were not interested in an exclusive photo deal. However, we will take some photos of the wedding on the beach, and post them on the 'Beech Boys' photo gallery. It should be a wonderful event!

Ship's Log

The moonlight helped us during the first half of the night, making it easier to see the waves. Winds dropped to 20 knots. The cabin was very stuffy last night, so I slept with my head by the main hatch to try and get some air, but tailwinds meant little air was circulating back into the cabin, as the door was in the lee. Winds were steady easterly at 20 knots, so we kept pushing on. At 9pm we only had 87 nautical miles to go before we reach 17°N 60°W. After this point there is just 100 miles to the finish!

We got some good meals sorted for the next few days - yum yum! We need to keep our focus and keep working hard - we're not there yet! James' back has been doing better each day which is terrific. My hat blew off when I stood up by the cabin and James made a brilliant catch as it flew past him while he was rowing! We thought 'Yorkshire Challenger' might have overtaken us, but although they have closed the gap to our surprise we were still 58 miles ahead of them.

Position at 9.00pm: 17°6'N, 58°29'W

24th March 2010

Beech Boys' Blog

Overnight we were bombarded with flying fish! Some literally missed us by inches as they passed over the boat as we rowed. In the dark, with poor visibility, it takes you by surprise when they flash past. Some flying fish didn't make it and crash landed on deck, flapping around leaving fish scales all over the place! The bigger fish, seven or eight inches long, are easy to see and hear as they flap about and we threw these back into the sea. However, the baby flying fish land silently and we had to tidy up these dead ones in the morning.

James had a very odd experience during one of his night-time shifts. In the still of the night he heard the thud of a fish crashing into the cabin door. However, despite a quick search James couldn't see where it had gone. He had just started to row again when he noticed my training shoe outside the cabin door move about on the deck! Was his fatigued brain playing tricks with him? On closer investigation James found that the dazed fish had landed in my shoe and in trying to get out, its flapping activity was moving the shoe! James kindly removed the fish before I put it on to start my next night-time shift!

The wind was still a favourable easterly today, although it had dropped down to 10 to 15 knots. On current progress we should be at the 17 degrees north 60 degrees west checkpoint by lunchtime tomorrow. This will then leave us with the final 100 nautical miles. It is amazing to see the chart and the plotted positions from all the days at sea and now we only have this last bit to complete. In the context of what has gone before it isn't far, although if you were going to set off to row 100 miles during the next two days you would think that was quite a long way! We are keen to finish and hope conditions remain good. It's certainly easier getting up in the middle of the night thinking, only a few more of these night-time shifts to go!

James' back has been gradually easing and he has managed to decrease the dosage of the pain relief. He is still going with the exercises and gentle stretching before and after rowing shifts, but gratefully he is so much more comfortable whilst rowing and moving around the boat now.

Joe the Swimmer and Bubbles would like to pass on their thanks for the good wishes they have received following the announcement of their wedding. They are very excited that we are getting closer and keep looking out for land! They would like to let people know there is no wedding present list, as they would rather a donation was made to WaterAid. Thank you.

A special thank you to Mark and Gemma Miles, Rebecca Robinson and Claire Holme. These GB athletes kindly ran in a relay race as part of the 'Beech Boys' farewell event last November. Thank you for doing that for us. You will be pleased to know we have the WaterAid shirts you signed for us on-board and we will wear these as we finish in Antigua.

Ship's Log

We have taken our favourite meals and snacks from our remaining rations so we have the best meals we can muster for the next few days. There are more sea birds about now and some different fish around the boat, which are about a foot long and quite dark in colour.

We phoned Christine and Lydia in Antigua, all is well. Lydia likes the Beach Club where they are staying and she told us to get there soon! Christine asked us what food we would like to eat on our arrival. What a great question to be asked after nearly three months of rowing!

The winds and waves have eased back so we can open the stern hatch on the boat. The cabin is once again pleasant to be in! We have been looking carefully at the detailed chart we have for Antigua, so we are up to speed with our arrival plans. Johan's weather updates show ongoing favourable conditions, so we shouldn't have to make unexpected changes to our progress. We are keen to finish and are pushing on as quickly as we can - now 68 miles ahead of 'Yorkshire Challenger'.

25th March 2010

Beech Boys' Blog

As the easterly wind became lighter through yesterday afternoon and overnight we lost a little bit of our boat speed. However, it was another good 24 hour run for us and we should reach 17 degrees north 60 degrees west by 1.00pm today. This is our last waypoint programmed into our GPS navigation system before we home in on the finish line at Antigua. We anticipate it will take us two days to cover these final 99 nautical miles, so we should arrive in English Harbour, Antigua, around lunchtime on Saturday 27th March.

The finish line is on the south side of Antigua extending one nautical mile due south of Cape Shirley. Although in our case there are no line honours at stake, to register an official race position we need to cross the official finish line. Needless to say we will be concentrating hard to avoid missing the line! Once across we will then have the final row into English Harbour itself. It is great to think of arriving and that is certainly a big motivator, however thinking of arriving doesn't put the boat on the finish line! We need to keep to our task, keep the oars moving and not get ahead of ourselves. As an extra boost we have gone through the final 10 days of food bags to get some additional treats to eat and keep the 'fuel' tanks topped up.

We have seen some new sea birds these past 24 hours which suggests land is getting closer. It will be brilliant to gain the first glimpse of Antigua some time on Friday. It will then provide a tangible target for us, rather than just a point marked on the navigation display. It is a pity the view to Antigua will always be behind the rower though, but it will be a clear signal of how close we are whenever we come out of the cabin for our next turn at the oars!

Christine and Lydia are on 24 hour standby to get down to English Harbour to see us in. They have a friendly taxi driver called Terry, who will pick them up at anytime, day or night, to get them there from their accommodation! On arrival, crews are provided with a meal on the quayside. We have an order in for fresh pineapple and cheeseburgers with salad and chips! It will be strange eating a meal which doesn't involve adding boiling water to a foil bag and then eating it out of the bag using a plastic spoon!

STOP PRESS - confirmation has now come through regarding Joe the Swimmer and Bubbles' wedding. It has been arranged for 30th March 2010 at 11am Antiguan time.

Once safely ashore we will continue with the 'Beech Boys' blog for a couple of days. This will enable us to relay news of the finish, how we adjust to living ashore again and details of the lifting out of the water of 'Beech Boys' for her to be packed up for the container ride home. We aim to have photos on our final blog entry of 31st March of us completing the voyage, as well as photos of Joe and Bubbles' wedding!

Ship's Log

Christine has emailed to tell us we have gained a race place having passed 'Ocean Summit', although we have not seen them. Rob and Stu who are rowing 'Ocean Summit' are both medics and Rob was scheduled to be the doctor on an imminent expedition to climb Everest. He has been taken off his boat on to the support yacht 'Aurora', so that he can get out to the Himalayas in time for the expeditions. Ash, a crew member from 'Aurora' is now rowing with Stu to the finish.

Winds were lighter overnight so our speed dropped back. The winds were not quite lined up with our course and our progress was not quite as fast as we would have liked in the afternoon. We did some rowing together in the evening feeling frustrated that we had slowed up - we know we'll get there we just need to keep ourselves steady and be patient.

Position at 9pm: 17°0.8'N, 60°11.19'W

26th March 2010

Beech Boys' Blog

We crossed 60 degrees west at 1.45pm yesterday. It was fantastic to be able to bring our final destination up on to the GPS knowing we didn't have another point to row to after we reached it. It is now a constant boost to us to only have double numbers on the distance to go display. However, 99 nautical miles of ocean is still a reasonable gap between us and the shore and with gentle winds yesterday afternoon and north-east winds overnight we still have plenty to do as we row across the wind and fight not to get pushed south of Antigua. The forecast is for easterly wind today which would be very helpful, but it has not quite arrived yet. At midday today we still have 65 miles to go - they may take a while to row!

During our approach to Antigua we have had a few interesting moments. Not long after going through 60 degrees west the sky was full of sea birds. They were in several flocks of around 20 birds and their squawks and cries and dives into the sea to catch fish provided us with something new to look at, as well as a noisy welcome to our final 100 miles.

Then a few hours later, a little after 5pm, James had a real surprise. The 'Marie Thomas', a bright yellow fishing boat, motored past on our starboard side! As you row you can't easily see behind you and the boat had approached us bow on, in what is a real blind spot for the oarsman. James shouted into the cabin where I was sleeping, "Come out quick with the camera, there is a boat out here!" The tone in James' voice communicated that something unusual was going on, so I scrabbled for the camera and made it on to the deck double quick.

As I emerged from the cabin I didn't know what to expect. Then I caught a glimpse of the 'Marie Thomas', a 30 foot open decked boat with a small wheelhouse at the stern. She was powered by two massive outboard engines. The whole experience took us both aback. We hadn't expected to see anyone out here and hadn't yet tuned into being able to see other people again. The two fishermen on-board were clad in yellow oilskins which only served to add to this surreal experience, as it was over 40 degrees Celsius!

As we both sat on deck we were intrigued that they didn't seem surprised to come across a rowing boat and we gave them a wave of recognition which they duly returned! They proceeded to throw out long lines with big pieces of bait on the hooks. It was great to watch them work together. There they were, less than 100 metres away. One of the men would haul in the line and the second man then used a large gaff to bring the fish on-board. Every so often we could see part of a fish still flapping and jumping around on the deck. They were big fish, three feet or more in length.

Our fishermen were joined five minutes later by another very similar boat, which was also engaged in fishing. Eventually the 'Marie Thomas' came over to us again and asked us where we were heading. They spoke in French and after a short conversation about fish and how many days we had been at sea, they sped off across the water! Their presence encouraged us that we haven't so far to go! They were the first people we had talked to without the use of our satellite phone or VHF since we had spoken to the crew of the support yacht 'Aurora' very early in the voyage and the only people we spoke to in French for the whole of the crossing! It was exciting to think it would not be long now until we would see Christine and Lydia again.

During the night we picked up a hitchhiker! Yes, we are getting close to land, but this particular hitchhiker was a small sea bird, which looked like a Tern. As I was rowing I became aware of a movement above the cabin and thought a flying fish had got stuck between the solar panels. Then the silhouette of a bird became clearer. Eventually it managed to sit on the cabin roof between the solar panels and the stern hatch. We guessed it was tired and wanted a rest, or just needed to recharge its batteries! It wasn't deterred by James taking a photo, or by James blowing the kazoo to try and move it on. It stubbornly remained with us until dawn when it decided to pursue a flying fish that skimmed past the boat. Never a dull moment out here!

We also had a few rain showers through the night. The half moon was bright in the sky and during one of the showers it produced a beautiful moon bow for us. This is similar to a rainbow, but due to the less intense light of the moon, a silvery white band is what you see, rather than the multi-coloured bow that is visible in the stronger light of the sun.

At our current speed we anticipate reaching Antigua late Saturday or early Sunday.

Ship's Log

Overnight a north-easterly wind, 15 knots took us south and we had to work hard to keep our course, rowing across the waves. Fortunately 'Beech Boys' is lighter these days and less water splashes on to us which is a bonus. I was glad of James' positive approach overnight, as I felt we were going slower and was concerned that if Friday's wind did not go round to the east we could be at sea another day longer. Rain showers cleared and after a cloudy dawn it was a very hot day again. We rowed together when we could in the afternoon and the wave pattern started to become more even.

At 1.30pm we spoke to Stu on 'Ocean Summit' via our VHF radio - he was about a mile away. They had been north of us overnight and better placed to use the north-east wind, so they had caught us up again. (We found out later they had rowed past us and had been within 250 metres of us, but we hadn't seen them despite them blowing their foghorn!) James spoke to Christine and Lydia on the satellite phone, who were excited about us arriving. 'Ocean Summit' should finish at a similar time. Evening sunset was good with some dark clouds adding to the drama. The winds moved back from the southeast to the east to push us along nicely. At teatime the oil tanker 'Aqua Chem' moved past us on a parallel course two miles to the south. We are both eagerly awaiting our first glimpse of Antigua.

Position at 10.30pm: 17°02.47'N, 60°58.2'W

27th March 2010

Beech Boys' Blog

As I rowed through my night-time shift I glanced over my shoulder every so often, keen to catch a view of our destination. It was on one of these checks that I started to make out a pattern of flashing lights ahead. I tried to make sense of what I was looking at. I narrowed down the options to a ship, a working platform with a cabin and lights on or a set of marker buoys! Nothing seemed to make sense though as it wasn't clearly any of these possibilities. I called through to James, who was sleeping in the cabin, "Has the AIS gone off?" James checked the chartplotter display. It did not reveal anything and after checking the chart for Antigua again, we concluded they were lights on communication masts on the island. This was to be our final day on the ocean.

As the moon disappeared below the horizon we were left with a darker pre-dawn sky. It was then, with that moonless sky, that we could clearly discern a lighter patch on the horizon ahead of us. It was Antigua! There was a matter of fact sense of, "Well, what did we expect to see?" There was an even greater sense of "this is it!" This was to be the day we would finally realise our dream of rowing across the Atlantic Ocean! We both knew that as the hours in the day ahead unfolded they would gradually draw to a close the prolonged hard work of the last two years.

We were on target, rowing towards Antigua, with 32 miles to go. James phoned Simon from Woodvale on the satellite phone when we were 20 miles out to give our ETA for English Harbour. We estimated we were on track for a 3.30pm arrival. This arrangement was part of the race rules, but we still felt slightly awkward phoning in the middle of the night to tell him this. Simon asked us to call 'Ocean Summit' on our VHF to let them know he had picked up their message on his phone. He hadn't got to it in time before it went to answer machine. Simon mentioned to us we needed to get further south to pick up the finish line, which we were aware of and appreciated his advice.

Overnight our boat speed was good and we decided to continue to row separately and get some rest so we could row harder through the daytime. After breakfast we set the boat up so we could row together. Only 12 miles to go now. We had some snacks to hand and James had his iPod connected to speakers on deck so that we could listen to our favourite tracks.

Our approach to Antigua was certainly exciting. The outline of the island started to take shape. The 'miles to go' figure kept counting down. After 81 days at sea it was wonderful to have our 'Beech Boys' "Land ahoy!" moment. It was also reassuring to see that the conclusion of our voyage was now in sight. The last race in 2007 had seen the average men's pairs boat make the same crossing in 53 days. Before we set off from La Gomera we estimated our crossing time would be 60 to 65 days. The further 17 days we had taken was an indication of the unusually difficult conditions the 2009-10 race crews had encountered. We had spent 10 days on para-anchor and other days just making far fewer miles than we had planned as we coped with crosswinds and headwinds.

We rowed together the last 12 miles and experienced two further wildlife encounters before reaching shore. At this time of year, humpback whales migrate from New England to breed in the warm water of the Caribbean. When we had eight miles left to row we saw one of these giants of the ocean make a couple of breaches. James saw it first and pointed to the splash so I was looking the right way to see it breach the second time. It was incredible to see the whale rise so spectacularly and majestically out of the sea. It then became a silhouette against the sky before descending with a huge plume of water back into its ocean home, probably half a mile behind us. It was truly a spectacular farewell to 'Beech Boys' from an Atlantic legend. A big whale was one of the things we had on our tick list of things to see before the end of the row! We felt very privileged. The wow factor? Absolutely!

If our humpback whale was waving us goodbye, slightly closer to shore we received a different message. A seven foot shark, light brown in colour, cruised along our starboard side. In case we needed it, this was a simple script note reminder to stay in the boat and keep rowing! Take the English Harbour exit.

As we closed in on the island a sport fishing boat was making its way out over the swell, passing 100 metres away to our port side. We waved across to them and they returned our greeting, the first of many we would receive in the next few hours. We adjusted our course to go further south. We had noticed when we stopped for a snack we were drifting to the north and we didn't want to miss getting round Cape Shirley. We continuously monitored our progress using the GPS repeater which was directly in front of me above the cabin door. There was no way we were not going to cross the finish line!

Once we reached 16 degrees 58 minutes north we headed due west. We were not surprised to come across fishing buoys now we were so close to land, however after passing the fourth set of identical red and white buoys, we began to wonder if we were going backwards! As we approached Cape Shirley, which is at the south of the island, we gradually turned to row parallel to the cliffs to make sure we were well inside the outer limit of the finish line.

As we rowed together and listened to James' iPod we talked about what our finishing time would be. As the race had started at 1.30pm, our finish time would be a day earlier if we finished before 1.30pm today. So from five miles out we worked hard to do this and maintained a very respectable pace. Then, with 1.30pm approaching, we realised that the finish line was 61°44.8' not 61°41', so there was a further 0.8 nautical miles to go! We wouldn't finish before 1.30pm and as we talked about this further we realised we hadn't allowed for the crossing of the time zones, as we had kept our watches on Universal Time, formerly GMT, since we started on 4th January. We did not mind. It had been terrific to row together with such spirit over those final miles. We called Simon on the radio to let him know we had one nautical mile to go - he said we'd obviously speeded up over the last few miles! We gave our ETA to the finish line as a further 15 minutes and eased up on our rowing.

We had a quick freshen up with some cleansing wipes and put on the WaterAid shirts that we had kept clean throughout the voyage. We knew photos would be taken at the finish and we wanted to use the opportunity to promote WaterAid. We also wanted to arrive looking half-decent! At 1.59pm we rowed through the finishing line at 16°59.2'N, 61°44.8'W to complete our row across the Atlantic Ocean. It had taken 82 days, 4 hours and 29 minutes. Tiredness, pain and muscle fatigue all fled from us, unable to stick around as the euphoria of the moment took total control.

The ABSAR (local coastguard) safety boat with Simon on-board met us at the line and together with yacht 'Mermaid' that had come out from English Harbour, with two other rowers Will and Tom from 'Heritage Explorer' to cheer us on, we were escorted along the coast to English Harbour. Simon confirmed we had crossed the line, and foghorns and cheers rang out. We now relaxed and the realisation of what we had achieved began to sink in. The row along the coast and talking to Will and Tom on-board 'Mermaid' was good preparation for what was to come. They told us it would be fantastic coming into English Harbour and it was!

Rowing along the coast we passed close to the cliffs which had a textured red/brown colour with strata picked out by the never ending work of the waves. The swell was taking things easy, just breaking gently onto the lower ledges of the cliff. Then ahead of us appeared the obvious, but narrow entrance to English Harbour. A small fort set on the cliff to the left of the harbour mouth was a reminder of its historic past. In Nelson's time it had been a strategic naval port.

The transition from ocean to sheltered waters was dramatic. The swell was left behind and the sea, chameleon-like, changed colour from dark blue to brilliant turquoise. Our entry to the harbour was like the opening of a door to a different world, where people lived in houses and plants and trees rooted themselves across the landscape. It was a sudden and magical change of environment.

As we progressed into English Harbour and our berth at Nelson's Dockyard, we weaved between the numerous yachts moored in the yacht basin. Now all that remained of our voyage was a few more rowing strokes. Those last few minutes represented a fraction of our time at sea, but were the basis of powerful and sparkling memories that we have since replayed in our minds many times over. People on their yachts began to shout across to us their greetings and tooted foghorns and waved flags. Small yacht tenders followed us in, some people took photos, a few people offered us meals at restaurants! It was truly memorable, a wonderful conclusion to our row. We kept saying "Thank you" and kept waving! It was made all the more special because we didn't know any of them and they just wanted to acknowledge our achievement. Smiles never left our faces!

Suddenly we could see the quay at Nelson's Dockyard and the crowd gathered there to welcome us. We were stunned when diners at the restaurant opposite our landing spot all stood up and applauded us. We had not been able to imagine any of this and it brought a lump to the throat! We both waved back to them and then I turned to search the faces on the quayside ahead of us for Christine and Lydia. It was an emotional and brilliant moment to see them among the waiting crowd. A feeling of triumph welled up as I saw them looking towards 'Beech Boys' and I shouted out, "I love those women!" Unfortunately they couldn't hear me with all the noise going on! But it didn't matter. I was going to be able to tell them again in a few moments!

The row along the Antiguan coast from Cape Shirley and the approach to the quayside through the yacht basin in English Harbour was the best part of the voyage. It was the sweetest feeling. Yet it would have meant nothing without everything that had preceded it at sea over the last 82 days and of course the two years of preparation that had put us on the start line.

The gap between 'Beech Boys' and the quayside was now less than 20 metres. The monotone noise of vuvuzela horns echoed around the harbour. Flares were set off and held high. They burned brightly sending out a stream of smoke. I shipped my oars and put them on the oar rest. James continued to steer, letting the momentum of the boat take us the final metres. I quickly coiled the bow line and threw it across to Simon and then we were alongside. Fenders were put in place by other crews that had finished before us and were now there as part of the welcoming party. It was a smooth landing.

Crossing the finishing line

We stayed on-board 'Beech Boys' as Simon cracked open a bottle of bubbly and we were then sprayed with a close range broadside of champagne amid cheers of celebration. As we stood there, we were soon soaked and Simon passed the bottle across to me. After a quick taste I poured some of it over James' head - well, he was wearing a hat! James took a swig and then returned the compliment and poured some over me - I was not wearing a hat! We hugged and congratulated each other before stepping carefully ashore.

We set foot on Antigua, and Christine and Lydia reached out to us and helped us keep our balance. We began the adjustment to life on land. The last time we had hugged was on a snowy Boxing Day at the departure gate of Leeds Bradford Airport. Now in the Antiguan sunshine nothing was going to stop us embracing and enjoying hugs and kisses, not even our champagne-soggy shirts and bristly beards! Simon shook us by the hand, congratulated us and gave us a hug as did other rowers - Dave Brookes from 'Team Panasonic', Will and Tom from 'Heritage Explorer', Mel from 'Explore' and Tony from the 'Team Insight' support crew. The steel band music played and to commemorate our arrival in the Caribbean we were both presented with a bottle of Antiguan rum by the Antiguan Tourist Board official. Temporarily it seemed as though we were at a wedding, with endless photos, everyone smiling and just amazingly happy to be together. It was a truly memorable experience and a fantastic conclusion to our adventure!

We walked with some very unsteady steps the short distance to the Woodvale Challenge marquee which was pitched on the grass by the quay. In the shade of the marquee was a table with two place settings. Waiting for us were two plates laden with our much thought about meal of cheeseburgers, salad and chips! It was good to use a knife and fork again and to have a normal meal. We had both put on a stone in body weight before the start, knowing we would lose weight during the voyage. We each finished the row two stones lighter as evidenced by our skinny legs. It was going to be fun eating well in the coming days and gradually putting some weight back on!

People Christine had got to know on the island over the previous three weeks came to talk to us. Staff from Alagana House, the villa where Christine and Caroline had stayed for two weeks, all turned up to see the rowers they had heard so much about. A family who lived on the island had been following our progress, as their children were keeping track of our journey as part of their school work. The children had drawn pictures for us and their grandfather had gone out with Simon in the ABSAR safety boat to take photos of us finishing. The contribution all these people made to our arrival was very special. It was such a great welcoming atmosphere!

Walking around certainly felt very strange. We were unsteady on our feet, our knee and ankle movements in particular were difficult to control. Provided we concentrated we managed to make a passable effort at looking normal, however if we allowed our minds to wander our staggering walk looked very comical! We had to get through Customs and Immigration before leaving Nelson's Dockyard and Simon walked round with us to the offices and talked us through what we had to do. It was with considerable pride that we viewed the official stamp marked in our passports. It read 'Arrived by sea'.

Having returned from Customs and Immigration without falling over or bumping into anything we checked that 'Beech Boys' was left tidy, with valuables taken off and thanked Simon for sorting things out on our arrival. Christine and Lydia led us off to find a taxi. We were soon heading for our accommodation at St James' Beach Club. The rooms were certainly spacious after the confines of our cabin and each had a balcony with a sea view. So we were able to keep in touch with the ocean in the event of having any withdrawal symptoms.

After a short time to shower and sit down, we made our way over to the restaurant for an evening meal. James and I were still no better at walking, so Christine and Lydia brought plates of food over to us from the buffet. It was wonderful to sit down and have a family meal together and begin the process of catching up with each other. At the end of the meal, I suddenly broke out in a sweat and felt faint. Adrenalin had long since deserted me, there was just no more energy left, or a refusal of the brain to try and find more. Christine asked a porter to drive us back to the apartment in the golf buggy. After 82 nights of rowing behind us, it was time to sleep for more than a few hours. Our mission was accomplished!

The instant my head touched the pillow I was asleep! Eventually I was woken by the sound of the palm trees being troubled by the breeze and the 'swoosh' of waves washing onto the shore. It took a few moments to work out where I was; after three months at sea these were unfamiliar noises. I had woken up at sunrise and the allure of watching the day begin next to a beautiful beach drew me out to the balcony. Christine followed me out and we sat there enjoying being together next to the sea. It was certainly a novelty sitting out in a warm ocean breeze and not having to row! I wasn't great company though. I kept dozing off to sleep!

The next few days were a peculiar mix of activities. We Skyped our families, sent news to our media contacts for their news reports and acclimatised to life ashore. Walking became a well co-ordinated activity, although getting up in the night to get a glass of water still required some care as initially the room seemed to be moving about! Simple things like being able to have a glass of iced water were luxurious, although it was interesting how after only a few days we started to take this as 'normal.' Fresh fruit and having a choice of food, rather than just what was in the day's food bag, was a real treat!

If we found some aspects of life ashore easy to adapt to there were plenty of reminders of where we had been for the last few months. On several nights I had dreams of still being out on the ocean rowing! James found it difficult to get back into a normal sleep pattern, sometimes waking at regular intervals through the night. Straightening the middle and ring fingers of my left hand continued to be painful. The grip strength for my left hand was really poor. Consequently, ice treatment and ibuprofen was needed for a while longer!

The day after we finished, we met Simon at Nelson's Dockyard to have 'Beech Boys' checked over. This was to ensure we still had all the equipment with us as specified in the race rules. We also had to clean our foul weather gear, life jackets, para-anchor and various ropes in fresh water to remove the salt. All the rubbish had to be taken off and the water tight compartments cleaned out. We also needed to repack 'Beech Boys' ready for shipping back to the UK. Despite having been at sea for 82 days, 'Beech Boys' looked terrific and not particularly different to how she was when we left La Gomera!

One morning at breakfast Lydia received a text from Simon. 'Yorkshire Challenger' was due in that day at 11.30am. We took a taxi to Nelson's Dockyard and met up again with Luke and Alex's families and other 'Yorkshire Challenger' supporters. It was great to see them in and we all went off to a local bar for a beer. One of the traditions is for rowers to write their names on the ceiling of the bar, which we duly honoured. It will be fun to go back at some point and see if our names are still there!

It would be remiss of me not to mention Joe and Bubbles, who had a wonderful wedding. The arrangements came together well, with Joe and his best man swimming to the beach for the ceremony. Bubbles looked gorgeous and wore a beautiful veil made by Grandma Morrow's bobbin lace group! It was a very moving occasion and certainly one to be remembered.

Once 'Beech Boys' was set up for the return trip and the wedding was over, it was at last time for a holiday! The beach loungers were waiting for us and much time was spent over the next few days lying on them, either reading a book or falling asleep!

'If I rise on the wings of the dawn, if I settle on the far side of the sea, even there your hand will guide me, your right hand will hold me fast.' Psalm 139:9-11

We Did It!

We set out to row 3,000 miles, to cross an ocean, to have an adventure, to challenge ourselves and to do something for other people we will probably never meet, who live on another continent.

As dad and lad, we became the first British father and son team to row across the Atlantic, or any ocean for that matter. James became the youngest man to row an ocean. Through WaterAid we provided for numerous people to have safe water and sanitation for the rest of their lives.

Through the row we visited some new territory as a family. It was the longest time Christine and I had ever been apart in 25 years of marriage. We had experienced the support of one another in a new way. Through tears, times of uncertainty, smiles and moments of triumph and the sweetness of being reunited, 'Team Beech' had pulled together. James and I knew all too well it had been a massive undertaking for Christine and Lydia to have the two of us out at sea. They are amazing people; they gave us the freedom to fulfil a goal that was alien to them, but for us was unachievable without them. It had been an extra ordinary two years of working together.

God had been close to us. We had grateful, thankful hearts, appreciative of a very special opportunity. The adventure of completing the Atlantic Job was accomplished. The adventure of the rest of our lives lay ahead.

As Charlie Kelly, one of the children at Coniston Primary School, wrote in a well done card to us - “You’ve rowed across an ocean, you must be over the moon.”

We made it!

Champagne moment

Team Beech Antigua

First meal ashore

Hoots of Praise

Hoots of Praise were sent via our blog to people who regularly sent us messages, did something special to promote the row, or raised funds for WaterAid while we were on the ocean. These were acknowledged on-board 'Beech Boys' with a hoot of our foghorn. Everyone listed below received a hoot of praise:

Katie and Hannah - thanks for telling us the dolphins we saw recently were Atlantic Spotted Dolphins.

The Murrays, Macosquin. Thank you for your encouragement via the email, and brilliant to know of the interest in the row from members at the Bann Rowing Club.

Marissa Phillips and parents Andrew and Sarah on the occasion of Marissa's dedication.

Lydia for passing her bio-med exam and then gaining third spot in the cheerleading competition at Loughborough with the squad from Sheffield University.

Johan Hoving - River Deep Mountain High for daily weather updates.

Andy Adamson and everyone supporting us from the COOLPilates Studio, Birmingham.

Sylvia and Cyril Dawson, Taff and Karin Bowles, Colin Hodgson and family, Julie Blaney, Alan and Glenda Phillips, Jeanie and Jez Woodhouse, David Taylor, Steve and Olive Crosby,

Woody, Sue, Billy, Joe and Daisy Wood and Rach, Mark, Tom, Matt and Dan Oliver. Many thanks for your regular messages. Ann Kite - for keeping our web page and blog info up to date.

Groups fundraising for Water Aid with us by rowing the same distance on their gym ergos - Lakes Leisure Ulverston, Greens Gym Sheffield with Vicky's rowing team and the group at the Munrow Sports Centre, University of Birmingham Sport. Brilliant!

Sandra Hoving - really good to have your box of surprises to open every so often.

Support from Coniston and across Cumbria.

Coniston Crusaders - fantastic messages.

University of Birmingham Sport - Zena Director of Sport and the Senior Management Team. Mark and Ann - help with communications. All the staff at the Raymond Priestley Centre for your backing and help. Sportex - Asker for nutrition. Jenny for psychology and Iain for encouragement.

Carl, Pete and Richard - Manufacturing and Mechanical Engineering for advice and practical support work.

Adam for your help at the University Open Days.

Everyone following our dot on the race site!

Guy, Jill and Olivia Pickup and Matthew, Nicola and Millie Rich - great messages.

Matthew, Dana and Rhianna from Coniston for your messages and interest in the row.

Daniel and Evannie - thanks for the poem and Yellow Submarine sea shanty - fab.

Vicky McDougall - Hunters Bar School, Sheffield. are raising funds for WaterAid. Activities include a non-stop rowing machine relay!

Janet Sullivan and family, Phil and Helen Glennon, Katie and DB, Jude and Doug for your regular emails.

Alex and team at University of Birmingham Sport.

Kat at WaterAid - thanks for your emails and encouragement.

Bobbin Lace Group, Coleraine, that Grandma Morrow goes to.

Probus Group, Highcliffe, that Grandma Beech goes to.

Dare and Joyce Holland, Steve and Cindy, Hannah, Esther and Isaac Chidlow for all your encouraging messages.

Helena Smalman-Smith, Kay and Don Shepherd, Duncan and Lindsay South - appreciate your messages.

Laura on passing your driving test - well done! Brilliant messages.

Cathy Edmondson, Ben and Angela Thorne and family - fantastic!

Keith and Ally, Craig and Katie Gibson, Senegal. Also, BJ Allatt - Australia.

Andy and Jen Ward, Glen at UBS for the emails on sleep Lorraine and David McGrath, Simon and Katharina Fisher, Chris McNaught and Luis de la Torre - St Nazaire Association.

Judith Hopkins - thanks for following our progress and for your messages, really kind of you.

Wendy Yates, Coniston Primary School, Mark and Elaine East.

Angus and Andrea Wightman, Rob Pugh, Eric, Jill, Lauren and Max Beech, Ian, Mindy, Vivienne and Allan Fowler, USA support group! Siobhan Winders and all at Pennington School.

Steve, Jenny, Andrew and Alexia Brockbank, Pete and Mim Kitts, Richard, Amanda, Craig and James George-Higgins.

Pat, Ros, Betty, Maeve and Mikey Callaghan - thanks for your support.

Ibby Brown - thanks for your emails to Christine which she passes on to us.

Chris, Ann and Sam Ensoll - terrific emails!

Andy and Penny Oxley, Judy and Ted - thanks for your support and messages.

Mark and Gemma Miles, Rebecca Robinson and Claire Holme. Thank you for signing our WaterAid shirts which will be worn at the finish. Mark and Gemma - thanks for your messages.

Christine and Lydia, as they wait for us to arrive in Antigua!